PRAISE FOR *YOU* *A FAILURE*

"*You're Not a Failure* sweeps the cobwebs of weariness from parents' souls and reminds them that they are enough, and not alone. Each page is overflowing with Whitney's heart-centered wisdom that we have come to know and love. This is a must-read for parents of tweens and teens."

—**Michelle Mitchell,** parenting educator, tweens and teens specialist

"Thank God for Whitney Fleming and her practical advice on parenting teens. As someone raising three (almost four) of them right now, *You're Not a Failure* is just what I needed."

—**Jess Johnston**, national bestselling co-author of *Here For It (the Good, the Bad, and the Queso)*

"With raw honesty and well-earned insights, Fleming unpacks the roller coaster ride of raising a teenager today. *You're Not a Failure* is the roadmap every parent needs by their side. After reading this book from start to finish, you'll want to keep it handy to reread chapters whenever you hit little bumps or giant potholes in the road."

—**Jessica Speer,** award-winning author of *BFF or NRF (Not Really Friends)*, *Middle School—Safety Goggles Advised*, and *The Phone Book*

"Whitney Fleming normalizes one of the most difficult times in a parent's journey. She shines a light into all the ugly and dark corners, allowing us to rid ourselves of the shame and frustration while at the same time helping us navigate it with wisdom and kindness. I am so grateful for this book and all of Whitney's work."

—**Asia Mape**, three-time Emmy Award–winning journalist, founder of Ilovetowatchyouplay, and the mother of three daughters

"In a world where we're constantly bombarded with confusing and guilt-producing messages on how to parent our teenagers the 'right way,' Whitney's book is a breath of fresh air. *You're Not a Failure* is filled with honest stories and insightful wisdom that cuts through the noise and chaos, providing reassurance and clarity. With humor that lightens the load and practical steps at the end of each chapter, this book is a must-read for any mom feeling lost or overwhelmed. Whitney helps us focus on what truly matters the most—the relationship with our teens. This book is a beacon of hope and support that *every* mom of a tween or teen needs to read."

—**Sheryl Gould**, parenting educator, author,
founder of Moms of Tweens and Teens, and
host of *The Moms of Tweens and Teens* podcast

"This book is a journey and an invitation through parenting the teenage years—through all the joys and missteps we're bound to face along the way. Whitney Fleming becomes the friend you can count on, no matter what. She tells the brutal truth and offers helpful tools to both maintain our sanity and build relationship with our growing kids as they wander through these difficult and beautiful times."

—**Mikala Albertson**, MD, author of
Everything I Wish I Could Tell You About Midlife:
A Woman's Guide to Health in the Body You Actually Have

"This book is full of golden nuggets that will really help you be the parent your teen needs as they cross the bumpy road to adulthood. It's raw, real, and full of practical things that will make a positive difference in your home."

—**Maggie Dent,** parenting author,
educator, and podcaster

YOU'RE NOT A FAILURE

YOU'RE NOT A FAILURE

MY TEEN DOESN'T LIKE ME EITHER

WHITNEY FLEMING

JB JOSSEY-BASS™
A Wiley Brand

Published by John Wiley & Sons, Inc., Hoboken, New Jersey.
Published simultaneously in Canada.

ISBNs: 9781394251988 (Paperback), 9781394251995 (ePDF), 9781394252008 (ePub)

For general information on our other products and services or for technical support, please contact our Customer Care Department within the United States at (800) 762-2974, outside the United States at (317) 572-3993 or fax (317) 572-4002.

Wiley also publishes its books in a variety of electronic formats. Some content that appears in print may not be available in electronic formats. For more information about Wiley products, visit our web site at www.wiley.com.

Library of Congress Control Number: 2024024161

Cover Art: © GETTY IMAGES | MIRAGE - C
Cover Design: Paul McCarthy

SKY10082730_082324

To my friends and followers on Facebook who encouraged me to write a book. I only pursued this outlandish endeavor because of your love and support.

And to every parent of big kids who feels alone in their struggles, this book is for you.

CONTENTS

CONTENTS

INTRODUCTION

*Our value as a parent is not the sum of our kids' accomplishments
and mistakes. It's the relationship we have with them and how
we both grow through it that matters most.*

–Whitney Fleming

M odern parenting is bananas.

There. I said it.

It often feels like I'm being pulled in different directions by the varying
parenting advice out there, and when I choose to do things differently or
go against the grain, I worry that I'm wrong or my kids may be hurt by my
choices down the road.

Basically, parenting an adolescent child is full of opposing guidance,
causing us to feel like we have no idea what we're doing. Some examples
include:

*Challenge your kids with rigorous academics so they get into a "good"
college, but also stay aware of their mental health.*

*Encourage your teens to find their passion, but club-level sports and
other activities will take up all your time and money.*

Set boundaries for your adolescents but let them be independent.

Connect with your teens, but don't force them to spend time with you.

Help them to meet their potential but let them make their own decisions.

Stay available, but don't solve their problems for them.

Monitor their tech but let them have their privacy.

Let them fail. Let them fail. Let them fail. But their actions have long-term consequences.

It all feels so confusing.

Add social media to the mix and it's like throwing kerosene on a bonfire. It seems like every post is about a kid who scored a 1600 on their SAT, made an Olympic development program for their sport, won the lead in their school musical, and discovered the genetic marker to cure cancer. Words like "average," "grade-level," "recreational," or "basic" are now negatives, and it's tough to encourage your child to do something just for fun.

If the comparison game isn't hard enough, you may also be dealing with an adolescent whose brain is going haywire and is making poor choices. They might be experimenting with drugs or alcohol. They might lie to you because they want to do what they want and don't like your rules. They might be doing poorly in school, staying out late, or lashing out at you. They might spend all their time at home in their bedroom.

And when big kids make bad choices, their parents face judgment from all sides. It can make parenting during an already challenging time feel even more lonely and isolated.

When all these things are in play, it can feel like every decision we make as parents can radically change the trajectory of our kids' lives and that they will miss out on a good life if we don't do certain things. There are times we will try to fix their mistakes because we don't want them to be penalized for what feels like our parenting shortcomings. We might try to solve their problems because our self-worth is tied up with their achievements and persona. We may try to engineer their life because of our anxieties.

It feels like so much and that we are never doing enough.

At the end of the day, you can feel so alone when you're sitting in your kitchen while your teen is brooding in their bedroom. You can try to do everything right and still struggle with the relationship with your teenager. You can give your kid your best, but they still may not like you. You can be raising a great teen but still go to bed each night feeling like a failure.

I don't think we say that enough.

So where do you go from here?

WE ARE NOT OUR PARENTING MISTAKES AND WE ARE NOT OUR KIDS' ACHIEVEMENTS

The funny thing about parenting is that just as you find your groove, everything changes, which is to say your kid continues to grow up despite your best efforts to keep them little. This hit me hard during the onset of my children's adolescent years.

On the outside it looked like my family had it all together. I had three beautiful, happy daughters, and I was the typical suburban mom driving her kids around in her minivan to all the things. Inside our home a different story played out. We struggled with communication and conflict resolution. We lost sight of our family values. We weren't always kind to each other.

If I'm being honest, we still struggle at times. Relationships are hard and to manage ones that are constantly in flux can be exhausting.

And that's really what is happening during these tween and teen years. You are trying to stay connected to someone you love who is evolving into a new person every single day. Your kids growing up is a universal truth that every parent must face and manage, and I haven't found many who have said it was easy.

I have been raising tweens and teens for the last decade. You may have seen me share my stories on social media as *Whitney Fleming Writes* or on my blog *Parenting Teens & Tweens*. While my Internet fame or viral posts certainly don't make me an expert, I do know this from my interactions with tens of thousands of parents over the years: we are all doing the best we can at the moment.

There is no manual for raising teens, so we can only parent the kid in front of us at any given time and grow with them. And sometimes, when we want to throw our hands up in the air and quit, the only thing we can do is look inward and work on ourselves.

I'm going to share my journey and the insights I've garnered as a writer who interacts with parents of teenagers every day, in the hope that if you are struggling, you can look at your relationship with your big kids differently. Each chapter focuses on a common challenge in parenting teens today and how I worked through it. The chapters are not laid out in order of importance as much as a chronological order of experiences for me. While I suggest that you read the book in the order it's presented to get the most out of it, there certainly are chapters—such as the sections on managing tech, middle school, and high school—that can stand independently.

This book won't give you step-by-step instructions regarding raising a teenager, but it will help you feel less alone in it. In sharing my story, I hope this book will:

- Help you cut out all the noise and chaos that the world is squashing down on you and focus on what is most important: the long-term relationship with your child.
- Challenge the expectations that outside sources are putting on our teens.
- Help you ask questions instead of fighting behavior.

- Enable you to gain control of your emotions so you can guide your teen through these challenging times.

Basically, I'm sharing my mishaps so you can avoid them—and carve out a connection with your big kids that lasts a lifetime. Perhaps you may even enjoy these teenage years a little bit more. My goal isn't to push one parenting style but instead to challenge you to create the one you need to be successful in parenting your kid, especially during the teen years. Sometimes we simply need to hear someone else's story to think differently about our own.

Whatever you're going through right now, whatever drove you to pick up this book—you are not the only one.

You are not a failure because you are struggling. This is hard.

We can grow through this together.

CHAPTER ONE

YOU ARE NOT A FAILURE IF YOU THINK RAISING TEENS IS HARD

Your success as a parent is not determined by whether your kids get into elite schools or prestigious professions. The real test of parenting is not what children achieve, but who they become—and how they treat others.
  –Adam Grant, organizational psychologist, college professor, Wharton School of Business, and best-selling author

I used to be a good mom—and then I had teenagers.

No, seriously.

As background, you should know that I had three kids in sixteen months, something I don't recommend. After three years of infertility, I finally gave birth to twin girls, and sixteen months later we added another daughter to our mix.

In order to survive, I was all about structure, routine, and balance. I was strict but fun (or so I thought). My kids (usually) listened, and while the day-to-day of raising three young children was exhausting, I thought we had it together.

They wore the clothes I bought, went to the activities I signed up for, and did their homework when they came home from school. They were fairly obedient, kind to others, and rarely talked back to me or their dad. In the grand scheme of things, I thought I was doing pretty well. I might have been a little smug.

And then, one day, I put three accommodating kids down to sleep in their bedrooms and woke up to tweens who had real feelings about life and how they wanted to live it.

The horror! It was bloody chaos.

That's when the wheels started coming off the bus for our family. My oldest two, fraternal twin girls with completely opposite dispositions, were entering middle school, and my youngest daughter was in fifth grade. That's when I started losing my way.

It happened slowly at first. Their middle school segmented students into specific groups and labeled some classes "honors" or "grade-level." Sports and activities became more intense, with week-long tryouts and auditions that would stress everyone out. The music department often leveled out kids based on capabilities, insisted on practice commitments, and suggested private tutors.

I felt the pressure both in my small suburban town but also on social media, news outlets, and conversations with my friends scattered across the country. Overnight, it felt like everyone was doing more and moving faster. I had friends whose children were attending prestigious camps to study science, running 5ks, or fundraising for important causes. There were middle school athletes already chasing national championships, state cups, and gold medals, and kids joining youth symphonies or starring in plays. One tween I knew had 50,000 YouTube subscribers, and another started a successful online shop.

I suddenly felt hyper-sensitive and aware of what others were doing around me, something I thought I had given up when I turned 40. While I once felt confident as a parent, I started questioning our family's choices and feeling anxious about their futures.

This icky feeling began creeping up inside of me. I thought I was doing right by my kids, but now that didn't seem enough.

I wanted to get back to basics and focus on what I knew was important for our family, but it was like I couldn't see how to get to the finish line from where I was standing. I didn't even know where the finish line was.

I felt lost in every way.

Even though my daughters were barely tweens, I started thinking about their upcoming high school experience and even about what college they might attend one day. It felt incredibly important that we carefully select what courses they took next, what activities they participated in, and how they spent their free time because it would heavily impact their futures.

I did not want them to be left behind or miss out, even though I had no idea what our end goal was. I kept wondering, am I pushing them too hard, or am I not pushing them enough?

As I came in contact with parents who were in the middle of raising older teens, I became more stressed about setting my kids up for what came next. I heard grumblings about taking enough AP and dual-credit classes, hiring tutors for SATs, and finding time for volunteer hours. Every sport and activity sounded like a major time and financial investment. Even the parents who I thought had it all together appeared frazzled, drained, and unsure.

It felt like the goalposts kept moving farther back, so I wasn't even sure what success looked like for my children anymore. Was it my kids getting into a top college? Winning a prestigious award? Earning a spot on an elite team? Or all of the above?

Where was the finish line? What does happiness even look like?

I started drinking the Kool-Aid. We heard from other parents that making a sports team at our large high school could be difficult, so when our daughters' teams disbanded because of a nationwide age-change ruling, we changed soccer clubs so they could play more competitively and gain the skills they needed to succeed. It was a strain on our family because practices were 30 minutes away and the program was more costly, but we committed to figuring it out because it seemed like it was in the best interests of our kids.

When I mentioned to a friend that I felt like I was passing myself on the road driving to all these practices, she shared that she took an extra job to pay for her daughter's competitive cheerleading program. I also found out that my neighbor's dad was volunteering at a concessions stand to offset his grandson's hockey payment. Another family I knew moved to a different district so their son could play football at a specific high school. It was way more intense and involved than the local recreational sports I played growing up, yet we felt it was something we needed to do.

In middle school, my daughter's orchestra teacher recommended we engage a private tutor so she had a shot of earning a spot in the higher-level symphony. We found her one who suggested she look at auditioning for a local youth symphony that was a few towns away. I couldn't imagine how to fit that in, but I was still considering it for some reason.

The icky feeling kept growing as I noticed a subtle change in how parents interacted. There was an edge to people wherever I went. It always seemed to be about what was next, how to push our kids to do more, how we were all exhausted, but no one wanted to be the one to say it out loud. The air always felt competitive even in situations that were more laid-back, such as back-to-school nights or fundraisers.

On the outside, I told my kids I only wanted them to do their best, enjoy themselves, and have fun. Still, I regularly checked their student portals, pushed them to practice, and stressed about their futures.

I was running myself ragged trying to work my job and maintain my kids' activities schedule, but letting off the gas didn't seem like an option. I wanted to be the parent whose kids were pursuing all the things they loved, but sometimes I wondered if they were doing these things to please me or themselves. And what were we gaining by being so busy and stressed all the time?

Meanwhile, inside the four walls of our home, things were starting to unravel. With three girls in the midst of puberty, I lovingly named our abode "The Little House of Hormones." My typically good-natured and accommodating kids had transformed into different people overnight.

My preteens didn't seem to appreciate all the things I did for them and resented the control I still desired over their lives. The more I tried to bond with them, the more they shrugged me off. I wanted to feel close and connected, and they wanted to spend time with their friends, on their phones, or in their rooms.

While the dynamic with my daughters was changing under my roof, what was happening outside my home was equally upsetting. As my adolescent children desired more independence, I struggled to control my anxiety about the state of the world we live in because so many things have changed since I was a teenager.

I felt overwhelmed by the proliferation of technology, social media, and recording devices everywhere. I worried about active shooter drills and gun violence, political drama and world strife, climate change and weather disruptions, mental health decline and rising suicide rates. We are still managing our health through the aftereffects of a pandemic, sifting through disinformation, and trying to understand racial and religious turmoil.

I was so tired of worrying about everyone and everything every second of every day—but I also couldn't stop worrying.

11

All this worry was in addition to what adolescents and their parents typically stress about, such as academics, peer pressure, their changing bodies, drug and alcohol use, social relationships, extracurricular activities, and life challenges.

Despite my best intentions, even with my kids' best interests at the forefront, even though I was trying my best at that moment, I could not get out of my head to see clearly.

And that pervasive ick feeling kept growing.

It felt like I was on a hamster wheel and couldn't get off.

I know I'm not alone. I co-own and manage a blog, *Parenting Teens & Tweens,* and social media accounts that reach millions of people annually. Many parents and caregivers in our online communities have shared that they feel the same way. It's hard to parent in such a complex and chaotic world. We are often so overwhelmed navigating the day-to-day issues of raising tweens and teens that we don't even recognize that we've lost our way.

I know I didn't. I knew what type of parent I wanted to be, but I felt captured in the eye of a hurricane and didn't know which way to go.

DEALING WITH THE CRAZY

I don't care what anyone says, adolescents and their parents have it harder today (my octogenarian mom agrees with me, by the way). There is so much to balance, and most of us are not emotionally equipped to deal with the stress and challenges we face in this modern world.

I've noticed that, as parents, we often respond to this chaos in a few ways:

- **We try to engineer our preteens' and teens' entire existence to set them up for their future.** We start sacrificing what was once important to us, such as family time, building life skills, connection, and self-care, in an attempt for our child to achieve some goal, like playing a sport at a high level, getting into a particular college, or winning an award. We start believing there is only one path to success, so we try to pave that path for our kids. Sometimes we're willing to bulldoze anything in our way to ensure our child's success.

- **We become terrified of making a mistake.** Instead of looking at personal stumbles—such as not making a team, getting a bad grade, or trying something new—as an opportunity to build resilience and grow as a person, we panic about how it will look or impact their future. It is why teachers get phone calls about a kid's low test score or missing assignment, why dads are screaming at teenage referees, and why moms are overly invested in getting their teens into a prestigious college. There are times when we are willing to sacrifice what our kids can learn today in the hope that they will have a better tomorrow.

- **We let our personal fears and anxieties get the best of us.** Sometimes we coddle our kids because we know that the big, evil world is scary, and that danger lurks behind every corner. We can't control the world around us, so we try to manage what is in front of us. I also believe that because the world feels harder than when we were kids, we indulge our children more. It's tough to be hard on your kid when we know that the rest of the world is pushing them down at every juncture.

- **We let our own trauma and personal disappointments cloud our judgment and impact our behavior.** Many of us walk around with emotional baggage we have never dealt with, and it often rears its head while parenting. It could be self-esteem issues, such as feeling we never met our potential or weren't able to because of reasons beyond our control. Or it might be because we were parented in a certain way that causes us to be ill-equipped to manage certain situations.

13

Some of us (cough, cough—me) are all of the above.

As someone who is a tightly wound, highly empathetic ball of anxiety who finds comfort in control, I struggle with separating my identity and emotions from my kids. I didn't want to parent out of fear, whether it was battling my own or instilling it in my kids. I didn't want to constantly battle my adolescents for control. I didn't want to sacrifice what they could achieve tomorrow because I feared failing today.

I wanted a different kind of relationship with my big kids, but why did it seem so scary to do things differently?

WHEN THE TIDES TURNED

There wasn't one specific moment that changed my parenting philosophy. When I started writing and sharing about it more on my social media pages, I found thousands of parents who could relate and wanted to change. When I started talking more with my husband about my struggles, he agreed we needed to shift our thinking. When I started questioning certain paths for academics or sports for my kids out loud with other parents, I found many nodding their heads.

We all felt that ick feeling but didn't know how to shake it. There had to be a better way.

What follows on these pages isn't clinical advice or research-backed tools. Instead, it's some lessons I've learned along the way from my first-hand experience and from talking to thousands of parents over the years.

Sometimes I look back at the beginning of my kids' adolescence, and I'm embarrassed. I'm ashamed that I became so preoccupied with the wrong things and lost my way. I'm sad that I sometimes missed the problems that were right in front of me. I'm disappointed that I got sucked into keeping up instead of leaning in. I'm heartbroken that I didn't recognize earlier how I needed to work on myself to give my kids what they needed.

But there's no place for these feelings in parenting. Our job is always to show our kids that we can course-correct at any given time, that we can have healthy conflicts, and that we can love unconditionally no matter what.

We can't solve all of our teens' and tweens' problems, but we can carve out relationships that allow us to walk together through them and grow up alongside them in the process.

It starts with understanding that what worked before in parenting may not work now. You may need to challenge your thinking, your beliefs, and maybe even your own upbringing. You must be courageous and willing to go against the grain of a society that is constantly telling us to push when what we may need to do is pull back. You need to have an unconditional belief that working on your relationship with your child will be what helps them succeed in this world, and not any accomplishment.

And you must never give up.

There is no one path to launch your teen successfully into this world, but if you can take a step back, dig deep into working on yourself, and open your heart to a new way of thinking, you can forge a new bond that will take you into their next stage of life.

I'm not saying it's easy. But I am saying that building a strong connection and relationship with your kids for the long game is worth it.

It starts with one brave parent.

MOVING FORWARD

- **Assess your current situation.** Are you happy or satisfied with the current state of the relationship with your teen? What brings you closer and what may be a distraction?
- **Analyze your decision criteria.** Often, we make decisions for our kids (and ourselves) out of fear that they'll miss out or get left behind. What ends up happening is we strain the relationship with

our kids today for fear of what they may miss out on in the future. (I discuss this more in the next chapter.)

- **Establish your family values.** We get so caught up in the rat race of modern parenting that we lose touch with what we value as a family. It's good to agree upon—or even put down in writing—family priorities so everyone is on the same page.

- **Self-reflection.** Understanding what makes us tick as parents, what motivates us, and what we may struggle with is a constant theme throughout this book. It may make you feel uneasy to dig into your past or analyze your behavior. I encourage you to lean into those uncomfortable feelings because that's when the change will happen, and you may start to think about things differently.

CHAPTER TWO

UNPACKING THE BOXES WE CARRY WITH US

Everything that is past is either a learning experience to grow on, a beautiful memory to reflect on, or a motivating factor to act upon.

–Denis Waitley, best-selling author of *The Psychology of Winning* series

I have some cardboard boxes sitting in my basement that I last looked at about 25 years ago. My mom dropped them off one holiday, and they traveled around with me for five moves across four states.

They sit on a wire storage rack gathering dust next to my husband's baseball card collection, which he swears is worth something if he could find the time to go through them.

To be honest, I'm not even sure what's in those boxes anymore. I know they contain some old yearbooks and news clippings from when I made our local paper a few times. There might be some class pictures and special art projects I made in my youth. I think there are some family photos, including a few of my dad, who passed away from lung cancer right before my twins were born.

Occasionally, when I venture into our storage closet to pull out some seasonal decorations or put some wrapping paper away, I admonish myself for not dealing with whatever is in those boxes. I know I should do something with the old photos, like frame them or pass them along to someone else in my family. Perhaps I could make a memory book of my middle and high school years for my kids to have as a keepsake. I know I should go through the photos, but even after all this time, it's still hard to file things away that have to do with my dad.

Something always stops me, and the boxes sit there like cardboard caskets of my past. There is always something more pressing to do, always a better way to spend my time, always something else I want to think about at that moment.

So those boxes remain a part of my identity, reminding me that I'm not yet willing or able to deal with whatever's inside.

UNDERSTANDING OUR OWN EMOTIONS FIRST

It's hard to unpack the boxes we carry with us, the heavy stuff that we don't know what to do with or may be difficult to let go of—the emotional baggage we take with us into every relationship.

We all carry around life experiences, former relationships, and events that define who we are in the now. This is most evident in parenting, when how we were raised often shapes how we parent our own kids.

When our children are young, we often adopt a similar parenting style as our parents used, but as our kids age, they often become emotional triggers, forcing us to deal with a flood of feelings about our past—regardless of whether we view them in a positive or negative light.

I came from a loving, middle-class home with two parents who encouraged me. There are parts of my parenting I incorporate intentionally from my mom and dad, and there are ways that I try to be drastically different.

Sometimes, I wake up to discover that I've carbon-copied patterns from my upbringing without even knowing it. I call those the circle-of-life moments. You know what I'm talking about, right? Like, when you walk into your daughter's room and it's such a mess that you tell her if she doesn't clean it, she can't go out with her friends until she does. I am pretty sure I heard that a minimum of 200 times between the years 1987 and 1991. I also may have rage-vacuumed outside their bedrooms a few times to ensure they were awake on a weekend morning, a trick I learned from my mother.

Or when your teen complains about your music in the car with her friends, so you turn it up a little louder and sing just a bit more off-key. My dad was the king of doing this with his Neil Diamond cassettes.

In those early tween and teen years of parenting my kids, there were times I exhibited behavior that I promised myself I would never do, knowing how they made me react when I was a teen myself.

Like when I expected my young teen daughters to obey without any discussion simply because I said so. I used to hate it when my parents did that to me. It was incredibly frustrating when they would not listen to an explanation or budge on their rules simply because them being right and me being compliant was more important than taking the time to consider how I felt.

There were also instances when my reaction to some typical teen angst and unsavory behavior resulted in my own intense emotional outbursts.

Looking back, I now know it was because I was stressed and anxious or sometimes because I felt undervalued and unappreciated. Overreacting and losing tempers were commonplace when I was growing up, and healthy conflict resolution was nonexistent.

I also was raised in an age when many topics were taboo. We never discussed issues like sex or the fact that many of my relatives struggled with alcohol. I didn't know how to communicate openly and honestly with my partners. I was unsure of how to get myself out of precarious situations.

I don't blame my parents for these things. They both came from fractured homes and did their best considering their upbringing. Despite some of our communication issues, I always felt loved and supported. I know they sacrificed so much so my siblings and I could have a great start in this world.

But it took me a long time to figure out what type of relationship I wanted with my daughters and how I needed to pivot to have them.

And while yes, some people have legitimate issues and trauma associated with how their parents raised them, many other factors from our past come into play that impact our parenting. Everyone has some baggage they bring with them from their past.

For example, some parents remember feeling not smart or athletic in school, so they live vicariously through their kids' achievements, unintentionally pushing and pressuring them to succeed.

Many people feel like they did not receive the attention or validation they desired from their peers or were bullied or left out in social situations, so they engineer all their kids' social engagements to ensure their place in a certain status. You can see this with elaborate parties or exclusive events or when parents go behind the scenes to ensure their child gets into a particular group or program or onto a specific team.

Some parents could not fulfill their dreams because life circumstances got in the way, so it can be challenging to let go of those ideas and support the person your teen is becoming instead.

Sometimes we don't want our teens to repeat the poor choices we made when we were their age, such as engaging in risky behavior like drugs, sex, or alcohol, sneaking out of the house, shoplifting, or something worse. The scariest part of raising teens is remembering the stupid things you did as a teenager.

And sometimes, our past becomes our present without our even realizing it—and it's our kids who pay the price.

It is why we constantly need to assess what's in the boxes we're carrying while we're in the season of parenting our kids in our homes. If these feelings become heavy, we eventually offload it onto them, and they start living *for* us instead of learning who they are and want to be.

I always say that my relationship with my kids changed for the better the day I started working on myself—and it is a long, slow, arduous process I must commit to every single day.

DO THE WORK

For most, parenting is an evolution; for me, parenting tweens and teens was a revolution.

One day, after what seemed like the millionth argument I had with one of my nearly teen daughters, I left the house without saying a word to anyone. I picked up a coffee at a drive-thru and parked my car in the empty section of a local shopping plaza.

And I cried. I did not have the relationship I wanted with any of my children. I barely had a relationship at all. I felt guilty for not giving them a better parent, one who would know how to handle these adolescent years better. I was angry at myself for getting constantly angry at them. I was emotionally drained with the mental load of parenting my older kids. I felt like a failure because I could not get the train back on the tracks no matter how hard I tried.

But mostly, it felt like I was the only one struggling to do this job that millions of parents had done before me. It shouldn't be this hard.

In that moment of despair, I realized I had a choice. I could muddle through these years, hoping we would both come out the other side, or I could do something about it.

It's not that I wanted to change who my kids were, but I did want us to have a different kind of relationship. I knew they were great people, and we could get along better. Maybe even enjoy each other.

So I latched onto the idea that you can only control your own thoughts and actions. I fought the chaos of the outside world by working on my mindset. I could love them through this hard time, but more importantly, I could learn to love myself harder.

I knew it wouldn't be easy. I'm a handful. But I was willing to do whatever it took to change my current situation. It's easy to say we would die for our kids, but can we change for them, address our issues, and grow as parents and human beings?

I was ready to try.

SMALL CHANGES HAVE BIG IMPACTS

I know what you're thinking. Isn't this a parenting book? Yes, yes it is, but as you will hear me say several times, every step I took forward in improving my relationship with my children started with working on myself.

Here are some steps that helped me grow.

Self-Care

While we often talk about the need for self-care while parenting, we have boiled that term down to solo trips to the grocery store or a mani-pedi every three months. It is so much more than that.

Self-care is the purpose-driven act of acknowledging your physical, emotional, and mental needs.

For me, that meant setting up a few boundaries within my family unit so I could focus on myself. Children (and some spouses) often think the world centers around them. When puberty hits, adolescents often become even more self-involved as peers become more important. Most tweens and teens are not developmentally capable of understanding the stress someone else is under or the demands of parenting while managing adult responsibilities. Many believe their moms and dads have an unlimited supply of time, energy, and resources like money (sometimes believing this until they have a child of their own). While it may seem like they're selfish, often it's simply a lack of perspective and communication.

At the onset of the adolescent years, I often felt frazzled, tired, and frustrated with my family. While my kids were striving to be more independent, it seemed like my schedule kept getting busier the more my kids' social lives and activities grew. Little things started to bother me more and the constant friction with my kids grated on my nerves.

Setting time aside to do activities that I found satisfying and soul-replenishing was great for my mental health, but I could not expect anyone else in my family to make them a priority. I needed to do it for myself.

There were times I would invite my family along to participate (hiking, watching a movie, etc.) and other times I did something by myself. They eventually learned that every person deserves some time to fill up their cup, and I learned that I am a better parent when I take care of myself. I also believe that self-care is an important life skill, and we need to model it for our kids so they know how to apply it for themselves.

I understand it can be challenging during these midlife years, for what some call the sandwich generation—caring for your kids and for your aging relatives. But if you can't control your temper, your reactions, or your thoughts, it's probably because you are mentally spent.

It's important to remember the old adage that raising little kids is physically exhausting, but raising big kids is mentally exhausting. You are worthy of self-care in both circumstances.

Understanding Your Triggers

If you open any book on self-improvement (of which I have read many), there is always a section on self-awareness. That makes sense, because self-awareness is the foundation for having healthy relationships. It is also the first step to changing behaviors you don't want to see within yourself to improve your life.

I always thought I was self-aware, but I confused that with being empathetic and able to see things from the perspective of others. I was good at behaving in a way that I thought others would appreciate and position me favorably in their eyes. To put it simply, I was a straight-up people-pleaser.

While I was great at projecting a certain image, what I did not know how to do was understand my thoughts and feelings and how those altered or controlled my emotional responses. When I took a step back to examine my behaviors around my adolescent kids, I started recognizing that I had triggers that caused me to respond in angry or irrational ways toward them.

Parenting triggers can be anything from lying and sibling fighting to disrespectful behavior and tantrums. I will talk more about managing triggers in Chapter 11 because it was a big way I helped improve my parenting and interactions with others.

Deal with Your Past Issues and Trauma

This one is so hard for so many of us. We must recognize that we are all walking around with unresolved guilt and grief for things that have happened to us. It might be how we were treated or an event we had to endure. It could be a crushing loss or trauma imposed by someone else. It could be something we did to a loved one or an illness that changed our lives forever. Those experiences always seep into our most important relationships.

I always thought I carried my baggage well, but I think what would be more accurate is to say I never unpacked it. I tucked it neatly in a corner and ignored it until the contents overflowed into my everyday life.

For most of my life, I didn't think I had the right to complain or be upset about things that had happened to me. I am lucky to have a loving husband, three healthy children, a roof over my head, and food in my belly. Talking about any past problems seemed petty and ungrateful.

But not acknowledging the pain I felt bubbling inside of me or addressing emotional issues I experienced often spilled over into my relationships in the worst of ways.

I carried unresolved anger at my dad for dying of smoking-related lung cancer, a preventable illness. I often felt anxiety about my health because of a freak illness I suffered from in my early 40s. I had complicated relationships within my family that caused constant tension. I was an empath who absorbed the pain and suffering of others, both strangers and those around me.

And because I never worked to resolve these feelings, because I never acknowledged the pain they caused me, because I never found closure, when they boiled to the surface, I took them out on others by overreacting, overthinking, and overresponding. I needed to get over my own issues to get on with becoming the best me.

Coming to terms with your past is a great way to develop a strong connection with your kids. It's also a productive way to ensure they don't repeat patterns.

Get Curious

In a famous scene from my favorite TV series, *Ted Lasso*, Jason Sudeikis talks about a quote, "Be curious, not judgmental." The premise behind his monologue is that we often assume we understand a person based on our preconceived judgments instead of asking questions or assessing a situation. It is a widespread problem when raising emotional tweens and teens.

Just as I was working hard to understand my feelings, emotions, and triggers, I had to work even harder to understand my teens. Instead of getting upset that they were snippy, I noticed that it often happened during a busy time at school or with one of their activities. When one of my daughters became forgetful and absent-minded, it was often because she was stressed. When another couldn't control her tears with me, I knew something else was happening in her life that I didn't yet know about or understand. I found the best response to their moods was not reacting, but digging deeper to find out the "why" behind their behavior.

Truth be told, they often didn't tell me what was going on, and that part was hard. I wanted to be a place where they could come to share their problems. But when I gave space and grace and let them go at their own pace, I discovered they came to me more often. That was a win.

I also reminded myself that they were behaving exactly as they should in this complex, chaotic time when their hormones were flaring, their appearance was changing, and their social relationships were evolving.

Their reactions were big and felt out of control, but their perspective on life was small. I needed to keep that in mind at all times. While they were tall enough to look me in the eye, they were still young and had much to learn.

Here's a mantra I often said to myself when frustrated: *Big kids have big feelings and need big love.*

Because of their developing brains, they couldn't yet understand their feelings or how to communicate them. Heck, I couldn't do it either as an adult.

So instead of reacting to a snarky comment because I thought it was personal, I started responding with "*Ouch*, it's not like you to be so mean. If you want to talk about something, let me know."

Instead of getting angry when they didn't do a chore or complete a task, I asked them, "Is there a reason you didn't do X? How can we ensure you get it done this week?"

And when they started getting older and wanted to do more independently, I used this simple phrase my friend shared with me: "What's your plan?" My big kids learned that they needed to think about how they would approach a situation before they asked.

Once I started getting curious, I noticed my irrational responses mostly dissipated. A simple question, "What could their behavior mean, and what could have caused it?" helps me to lead with compassion and grace first instead of needing to apologize for my behavior later.

And instead of thinking they needed to grow up and act more mature, I reminded myself that I was already grown up.

Develop Healthy Coping Mechanisms

I use the phrase "coping mechanisms" with my teens all the time. They love it (insert sarcastic eye roll here). But honestly, if I had the authority, I would create a mandatory high school class solely on coping mechanisms, because most of us have few or none.

Coping mechanisms help us deal with stress and unpleasant emotions, and there is a lot of that when you are raising adolescents. What I love about them is they are an active way to gain some control over your life when you feel like everything is uncontrollable.

There are many ways to develop coping skills. Some are as simple as deep breathing and self-talk, and others are more intensive, like taking a class or attending therapy.

My personal favorite is taking an outside walk every day possible. It's good for my mental health, and my dog likes it too! I'll discuss the importance of coping mechanisms in Chapter 10.

Let Go of Resentment and Martyrdom Motherhood/Parenting

We talk about this so much when our kids are younger, but I don't see it discussed as often during the tween and teen years. While the season of raising littles is physically exhausting, the next season is mentally draining—and kind of annoying.

Helping your adolescent become independent is no easy task. On one hand, there is still so much manual labor—a house to clean, errands to run, and dinners to cook. On the other hand, you know that time is running out, so you try to help your kids become capable adults by teaching them the life skills they need to succeed in the real world.

And our teens don't seem to appreciate that we are working so hard behind the scenes on their behalf.

We are still in the muck of raising them while they desperately try to cut the apron strings. It can be incredibly frustrating to hear "I know" 50 times a day when you feel certain that they do not know.

I had to work hard to separate their behavior and choices from my expectations. I could not make them feel a certain way, make them like something, or make them want to do something. There were basic rules of conduct, but I also had to realize that their desire for a life outside of my orbit was natural.

I also had to recognize that there is more than one way to skin a cat. Maybe they did not load the dishwasher the way I wanted, cut some corners on a school assignment, or worked a different type of part-time job, but the lessons come from the doing, not from me telling them how it was supposed to be done.

Most importantly, I had to painfully accept that I could not force the relationship I wanted to have with them. While some parents say that their teens share everything with them, I came to terms with the fact that it was okay—in fact, extremely healthy—for my daughters to keep some things private.

It was a harsh realization, but I believe in the premise that our relationship has to be on terms that benefit us both, not just me.

I also learned not to use guilt as a weapon. Making your tweens and teens feel bad to get your way is not the best tactic for keeping a long-term relationship. This was something I did at times without recognizing it.

Gratitude, Gratitude, and More Gratitude

I'm the first to admit that I used to find gratitude a little hokey. Like meditation, yoga, and other things I didn't understand, I thought practicing gratitude was something for other people. And then I was raising tweens and teens. When you feel like you're facing a roller coaster of emotions with your adolescent children each day, it can wear on you. It's easy to start expecting to see certain behaviors out of your kids or lose your ability to give some grace. Gratitude can soften the edges of those highs and lows and bring some peace to the chaos.

Practicing gratitude helped me discover that spending time acknowledging what I loved about my kids is more important than pointing out what they're doing wrong.

In those tween and early teen years, I was simultaneously going through a few health challenges. It was so much easier to see the negatives in every situation and person than it was to see the positives.

I was in a bad mindset and a dark place. I felt like my kids were constantly pushing my buttons. I felt stressed and overwhelmed with decisions. I felt like I was pulled in a million different directions.

My negative attitude became my default and a fight with one of my kids was like a self-fulfilling prophecy each day. I knew it was going to happen, so I was constantly on the edge.

It was unhealthy for my entire family, yet I couldn't get out of my own way.

One day, I read an article that included a link to a gratitude app I could put on my phone to write down three good things about each day. The goal was to retrain your brain to notice the positives in your life, instead of the negatives.

I needed this. I decided that for 30 days, I would write down one thing I loved about each of my children at the same time every day: 9 p.m.

It seemed ridiculous at first, almost immature, but I knew I needed to embrace something different. Sometimes after a long day of battles, it would be harder to complete the list than other days. During a week where I butted heads with one of my daughters daily and she was ferociously angry with me, I had to dig deep to put something on that list at the end of a long day. On other occasions, I felt too busy to focus on it or it seemed silly because I was in a good mood. But I kept going and completed it every night by 9 p.m.

Damn if it didn't work. The simple act of writing those things down slowly changed my mindset. Instead of waiting for one of my daughters to walk into a room like a tornado, I would look for the good qualities. I started handing out more compliments and less criticism. I felt calmer when around them. In fact, I felt calmer in general.

Typing those simple words daily into my app helped me focus on my daughters' amazing attributes and notice other things in my life I should appreciate. It enabled me to approach problems differently and helped me maintain perspective on what was important to me in parenting—and what was important to me in my life.

And as my attitude started to change, something incredible happened. Their attitudes started to turn more positive, too. The snark somewhat dissipated. The exasperation diminished. The battles were minimized.

I saw things more clearly and could control my reactions better.

It wasn't perfect, but it was a little more peaceful, which was a big win in my book.

LEARNING TO LEAN IN

I can honestly say that I've grown the most as a person during these years, parenting my tweens and teens. Clearing my head and learning how to unpack and address my issues has helped me to understand why I respond to my kids' behaviors in certain ways, and it has helped me connect to them on new levels.

Most importantly, instead of giving myself distance and running away like the few hours I spent in an empty parking lot, I have learned to lean into my kids' emotional needs. I can do that now because I can better manage my own. And in doing that, I get to know—and love—my children on a deeper, more personal level.

It's not always perfect, but it's a preamble to what I hope is a long love story of connection to my kids throughout their lives. It is a revolution that I hope never ends.

MOVING FORWARD

- **Unpack your own emotional issues.** Take the time to understand if you're carrying around any unresolved issues from your childhood. Ask yourself questions like "What did I like about how my parents raised me, or what didn't I like?" or "What issues from my teen years may impact how I view my teenager?" Understanding our own emotional baggage can help us be more objective in looking at our children.
- **Do the work.** If you recognize that your past issues are impacting the relationship with your teen, it's up to you to do the work to address those, either by talking to a professional or working on identifying and managing those feelings.

- **Create new habits.** Raising an adolescent in today's complicated world can feel like a lot, and an important part of preparing your child to launch is modeling self-care, emotional regulation, and coping mechanisms. Take the time to find the tools that work for you so you can help your child navigate the rocky road of these years. It's like the advice an airline crew provides preflight: "Put on your own oxygen mask before helping others." We must take care of our own well-being before we can help our tweens and teens with theirs.

- **Lean in and love harder.** You may be tempted to take a step back during these years because they may bring up old pain or feel too overwhelming. I encourage you to lean in and take the time to heal your hurt so you can help your kids—and yourself—become the best version possible.

CHAPTER THREE

MIDDLE SCHOOL IS THE WORST

One day, middle school will end and become high school, and after that, it just becomes life. All those things you think are important now won't be anymore.

–Jeff Kinney, author of Diary of a Wimpy Kid

I have this great photo of me in middle school in all my puberty glory. I'm wearing not one but two colorful Swatch watches (one from Santa, the other I received for my birthday a month later, along with a cool rubber face protector). My bangs are teased up high from a combination of Aqua Net, a hair pick, and my Conair curling iron. I have a striped Coca-Cola rugby shirt on with the collar pointed up, and I'm guessing my Guess? jeans on the bottom. I look so happy, maybe even kinda cool.

But the truth is, middle school was a tough time for me. I acquired a womanlier figure in sixth grade and put on some weight. I remember feeling uncomfortable in my new body and acutely aware of what other girls looked like. I fought bouts of acne and thought that I never had the right clothes, right hair, or right bag. I moved states twice, and the sting of standing out as the new girl stayed with me. I desperately wanted to fit in, but I was always on the periphery of the cool kids. And I was a little boy-crazy—I wanted their attention but had no idea what to do when I received it.

Middle school was also when I became incredibly self-conscious about my parents. I did not feel I could talk to them, and I certainly didn't think they could understand my life. I found them irritating and avoided them at all costs. I started closing off, and my mom started enforcing more rules, so there was a constant push and pull.

It was during this period I started getting a little sneaky and obstinate. I knew my parents' rules and boundaries, and I knew how they would react if I broke them.

It was the same dance every time. I would do something wrong and try to get out of it either by omitting some facts or telling a white lie, and my parents would catch me and yell and lecture. I would cry; they would yell more. My dad would soften, making my mom more rigid with her rules and punishment. This happened over and over again and again for a good portion of my tween and early teen years.

I was a good, strong-willed kid who pushed limits, and I now know my parents were living saints to deal with my insufferable attitude during that time. They were dealing with their own midlife struggles: my father was forced into early retirement when his company was sold, my mom faced some health challenges, and one of my older siblings made some unfortunate choices that broke my parents' hearts.

And there I was, thinking the whole world revolved around me and whatever problem I had when I woke up that morning.

It's hard to pinpoint now, but I believe I felt so uncomfortable in my skin that everything made me self-conscious. I also did not have someone to talk to during that awkward time to understand better what I was going through and how to handle it.

Luckily, I made it through relatively unscathed, and my parents did not kick my butt to the curb as they rightfully could have based on my attitude. But I remember that period of my life as hard and heavy and unenjoyable.

And then, a few decades later, I realized that the only thing harder than going through middle school was being the parent to a middle schooler.

SEVENTH GRADE SUCKS THE WORST

The turning point for me started when my kids hit seventh grade.

Let me preface this by saying I've been called a naysayer about middle school. Some people have said I should be more positive or at the minimum focus on the positives because there are some good things. I appreciated my kids' teachers, and I enjoyed some parts of them growing up during that time.

But truly, seventh grade is the absolute worst. My unscientific anecdotal feedback from other parents tells me that this is true in many other homes as well.

I know this is a strong statement, but I couldn't wait for it to be over for my kids. There was so much drama emerging from multiple sources. There was more homework, changing friendship dynamics, and a sudden interest in romance and gender identity. It's when phones and social media never stop being a problem, and parents stop talking to each other as much. It's when kids can be the cruelest without even realizing how cruel they are. It's when some sweet kids are so awkward that it's almost painful to watch. It's when you can no longer protect your babies from the outside world.

Middle school brought out the worst in them. And it brought out the worst in me.

During seventh grade, one of my daughters and I started to develop what I can only describe as a tenuous relationship. Our dynamic changed slowly. First we started arguing about the trail of stuff she left all over the house, like dirty dishes, sports clothes, and papers. Then there were some minor fibs and disrespectful behavior. And then we just started to battle over every small thing.

The two of us had a dance we performed nearly every single day for months. I would pick her up from school, practice, or a friend's house. The post-event conversation would start cordial and loving, and then it would make a 180-degree turn faster than a knife fight in a phone booth.

It usually went like this. We would be casually chatting about her day when she would bring up a topic we needed to address. I would ask if she finished her homework, completed a chore, or followed up with a teacher. She would sigh or roll her eyes and then sarcastically respond, "I'll do it." Instead of keeping my lips zipped—*like I knew I should*—I would then toss the next grenade.

"And it would be great if you would pick up your stuff. You need to be more responsible." To which she would reply, "I *know*! I told you I would do it." Then it would go from bad to worse as we rehashed whatever problem we were having at that moment.

There were so many missteps. She could have been more honest, and I pressed her at every opportunity. She would make promises she had no intention of keeping while I continued to make threats. She was growing moodier, and I was growing tired of her attitude.

Sometimes the disagreements would get personal, and even now my cheeks flush with shame as I recall some of the words that flew out of our mouths. I would question her effort when I saw that she was not performing up to her ability on the soccer field, thinking it was a sign of the apathy I was witnessing from her in every aspect of her life. I questioned her desire to be successful and meet goals when she told me she forgot about her homework or didn't study for a test. I questioned her love for the rest of the family as I admonished her for the messes she left around the house. I questioned her morals when I caught her in some lies.

Sometimes she would respond in kind, cutting me deep precisely where it hurt. She would ask, "Why can't you be like other moms?" "Why are you so hard on me?" or "Why do you care so much?"

I know these sound like silly little things, and I know deep down they are. But it was the enormity of so many small issues that seemed to break me down. As a first-time mom to an adolescent, I couldn't help but think that if she was lying about the small things, if she couldn't adhere to simple rules, if she couldn't come to us with something minor, how could we trust her with the big stuff? It was about the totality of our relationship, but it was always something minor that set us off.

My husband and I tried punishing her and taking things away. We encouraged and rewarded good behavior. We had endless talks about responsibility and acting as a contributing member of our household. But nothing seemed to work. We could not get through to her.

When I think of this time and read these words back, I know what I was doing was wrong, but in that moment I couldn't see it or get out of my own way.

One day I had an incredibly stupid battle with my daughter about the state of her room. The thing is, the fight was not about her disaster of a bedroom. It was about the fact that I did not like her attitude about anything lately. I was not too fond of how she spoke to her sisters earlier that day, how she rolled her eyes when I asked if she could walk the dog, and how she didn't put her laundry away like she said she would. Again.

I was particularly frustrated because it seemed like she didn't care about helping me even though her sisters were putting forth effort—and even covering for her at times so she wouldn't get in trouble. This was after catching her in a small lie about a friend and a few other issues earlier in the week.

So when I walked in and saw that she hadn't picked up her room like she promised, I lost it. I'm not proud of how I acted. I belittled her and dropped a few cuss words. I shamed. I became an unrecognizable person. It was like I had an out-of-body experience. I was just so frustrated. I could not figure out how to get through to her.

While I acted immaturely, her behavior was much more aligned with her age. She tried to fight back and had some choice words of her own for me. But what truly scared me was the fire I saw in her eyes that was never there before, an anger I didn't know she had within her.

It ended as badly as it started. She was crying; I was enraged. I stormed out of the room in a fury; she slammed things around in her room.

We spent the next few days barely speaking to each other. When I dropped her off at soccer practice later that week with a new team she had joined a few months prior, I watched as she put on her gear away from most of the other girls. As the players paired up to start warmups, she tied and retied her shoes and looked for something in her bag. Finally, a young girl who arrived late came over, and I watched as my daughter slowly walked out onto the field to kick with her.

I decided to stay and watch the practice, and that's when my heart broke into pieces. The team was disjointed and cliquey. The other players mostly ignored her. The daughter I was beating up at home looked sullen, awkward, and nervous, utterly different from the vibrant kid excited to play just a few months prior.

Later that night, I asked her about the practice and what I saw. When she shrugged it off, I softly said, "I saw it with my own eyes, kiddo. It didn't look like a great experience for you."

The dam broke, and a flood of emotions rushed out of her tiny body. I do not think I received all that was happening, but the gist was that it was not going well, and she didn't feel like she was fitting in with this new group. She was younger and smaller and struggling to find her place. None of the girls attended her school, and I don't think she received a warm welcome.

The team was large, and every girl was fighting for a starting spot and playing time. My daughter explained that there were a few groups of girls who played together in the past or knew each other from school, and then there was her.

She explained, "It's not that they're mean to me, but they're just not nice either."

It was like a sock in the gut. When my daughter was already feeling at her lowest, I kept pushing her down farther instead of extending her a lifeline. While there were things we needed to work out, I certainly was not handling our issues effectively.

As I lay in bed later that night feeling awful, I wondered how I missed the signs. Her behavior had worsened since she started with this new team, and although it didn't explain everything, it made sense. What I chalked up to disrespect was actually her experiencing something new and not knowing how to handle it. All those emotions needed to go somewhere, and I was the perfect target.

After that night, I also recognized that she struggled with her communication skills and that asking for help was difficult. She was also easily embarrassed and accustomed to being one of the better players on her team, so this probably heightened her anxiety to new levels.

What I knew for sure was that it wasn't surprising she didn't come to me for support. She was facing some uncomfortable situations, and our recent blowups were just another reminder that she was not enough—for her team or for me.

I spent hours driving her to practices, games, and tournaments. Still, I didn't spend a minute trying to understand her recent behavior. I focused on the "what" she was doing and how it impacted me, instead of the "why."

If you were on the outside looking in, you would not know what was happening. She was a strong athlete and capable student with a loving and engaged parent—but we were in a spiral, and I needed to pivot.

WHEN YOU'RE IN THE EYE OF A HURRICANE, YOU CAN'T ALWAYS SEE THE DESTRUCTION HAPPENING AROUND YOU

The hardest part about seeing how far I had veered off the rails as a mom—and knowing how much I had hurt my child—was that this was her first introduction to conflict resolution. Not only did I not dig deeper into what was going on in her life to understand her perspective, but I took an oppressive stance, expecting her to listen and obey me simply because I said so and was the authority figure.

I did the exact thing that pushed me away from my parents as a teenager, even though it was the complete opposite of what I wanted to do. I was not exactly the calm, compassionate, rational mother I always hoped to be. I did what I disliked simply because it was all I knew.

The difference was that in middle school, I was clear on my parents' approach to discipline. They told me the expectation, and there would be consequences if I didn't obey.

I wanted to be a different kind of parent to my three children. I wanted to incorporate the best of my upbringing with some improvements. I did not want to be a doormat for my daughters' bad behavior, but I did want to be a parent who listened, respected, attempted to understand, and led with love.

I told them that they could come to me with anything, but my actions spoke differently.

Something had to change.

OUR RELATIONSHIP WAS LIKE A BLISTER

A blister happens from friction: constant forceful rubbing.

That's what was happening to me and my young teen daughter in middle school; we constantly rubbed each other the wrong way. Our relationship was a gigantic blister, and it was hurting us both.

Her behavior made me so frustrated that I pushed her on everything big and small. I needled her about her room, her attitude, her schoolwork, her lack of awareness for others, and her inability to change. The lines blurred between her actions and who I told her she was as a person.

Whenever I confronted her she started circumventing the truth and shutting down. She retreated to her room at every opportunity. She pushed back when I wanted to connect. She tuned me out when I lectured.

If you've ever had a blister, you know it doesn't go away overnight. You can try Band-Aids or use ointment, but the only course of action to ensure it doesn't happen again is to stop doing what caused the blister in the first place.

Stop the friction and heal the blister.

When you're dealing with an emotional mom and a hormonal teenager, this can be harder than it sounds. But I was so tired of the constant friction; I was tired of feeling like a failure; I was tired of watching my daughter hate to be around me; and I was tired of hating myself after every interaction with her.

I wasn't sure where to start, but I knew it began with me. I made a conscious decision every morning determined to control how I interacted with my daughter.

Was I going to nag her about her bedroom, or could I let that go?

Would I question her every move, or trust her ability to get things done?

Could I give her the benefit of the doubt when I knew she was ignoring me, give her grace when I knew that's what she needed most, and have an unconditional belief in the goodness of my sweet daughter?

Could I control my responses, could I look deeper, and could I be the mom I wanted to be to my kids?

The first day of my new parenting initiative didn't go well. She was running late in the morning and forgot to make her lunch. Instead of lecturing her, I threw a few things in a bag and left it on the counter for her.

Because she was stressed, she was snarky to her twin sister and then to me. Instead of engaging, I simply asked her to stop talking until she could be kinder to us. She rolled her eyes, and I ignored it.

When she walked out the door without saying goodbye, I was thankful that we got through the morning without a mother-daughter tornado touching down in our kitchen because I was getting close to imploding. #winning

TAKING AWAY THE FRICTION IN A RELATIONSHIP

While she was at school, I wrote down a list of non-negotiable things in our home—tasks and responsibilities that were essential to being a part of our family. It included basic care of our dog, keeping food and dirty plates and utensils out of her room, cleaning up after herself in common areas, speaking respectfully to family members, adhering to tech guidelines, and informing mom and/or dad of her whereabouts.

My second list comprised things that I would no longer poke her about, such as the state of her room (excluding dishes/food/garbage), daily school work (I vowed to check the portal every two weeks and let her figure out when she would do homework or study), incessantly reminding her about things she needed to bring to school or practice; clothing choices (like not dressing appropriately for cold weather), eye rolls (my daughter told me a few years ago that she didn't even realize she was rolling her eyes most of the time), repeated lectures and reminders, and engaging in arguments that had no point.

Writing it down on paper enabled me to see how dumb most of our arguments were. I recognized that while my daughter's behavior was somewhat volatile and unpredictable, I now had a plan and could make a choice for every interaction with her. I could not control her behavior, but I could control mine, and that was a significant first step.

I started helping her more without expectation, even when I knew she could do most of these things herself. I would put away her laundry or bring some stuff to her room. I ignored the fact that she did not share an event that happened at school, even though I learned about it from her teacher. I rinsed off the peanut butter spoon in my sink, even though it drove me crazy. I let her siblings work out their issues with her directly.

While my daughter was a diligent student, I noticed she struggled with organization. Instead of getting frustrated that she left papers and books around, I put them in a pile outside her door because her desk was too cluttered. One day I bought a few organizing containers for her to put things that were always on her desk and left them on her chair with a note: "Thought you could use these. Love, Mom."

It took a few weeks, but one Sunday she spent the entire day clearing off her desk and putting a few things in the holders and baskets. After that, she started completing her homework in her room, where she could keep everything in one place. Even though we had talked about this so many times, she needed to take ownership of it and do it on her terms. I ignored the clothing scattered all over the floor (my friend calls it a floordrobe) and the counter in her bathroom that looked like a CVS explosion.

Another day she came home in a mood, and I could feel the tension in the air like humidity before a big storm. I was tired too, so after the third barb she threw at me complaining about something, I calmly stated, "I think we should end our conversation here, but if you need me to help you with something, just let me know. I'll be in the other room."

Nuclear meltdown avoided.

Our new dance reminded me of when I put my kids in time-out as toddlers. The punishment was supposed to be a consequence for them, but it helped me calm down and avoid any irrational behavior.

Ninety-five percent of our problems were simply about diffusing our emotions—hers and mine.

It felt a little contrived and calculated at first, and yes, even awkward. There was a constant tension in the air because this was not natural for either of us. But I avoided barraging her with questions about school, her friends, soccer, or, honestly, anything personal to her. I tried to respect her middle school privacy and accepted that she did not want to share that part of her life with me at this time. I constantly reminded myself that she was a great kid and to believe the best in her. As long as I felt like she was safe, I backed off.

It hurt, and I felt rejected, but I did my best, with a few minor missteps, to give her space. Instead, I often extended invitations for her to go for frozen yogurt, cook a meal, or watch a show. If she didn't want to go, that was fine. If she did, I would make small talk unless she mentioned something she wanted to discuss.

I kept at it for several months, well into ninth grade. Sometimes I helped her, and sometimes I let her fall. Sometimes I forced a hug so she could physically feel my presence, and sometimes I let her dictate the terms of our relationship. Sometimes I let a terse word or action roll off my back, and sometimes I simply said, "Please leave the room if you are going to behave like this."

We gave her more options. She decided to switch back to her old soccer team and even picked up a new sport. We let her face more natural consequences when it came to school, so she learned the importance of responsibility. We gave her more latitude for her attitude, knowing she needed to figure out the complexities of her emotions, and kept in mind that there was likely a backstory behind her demeanor.

We worked on building trust. We found that most of my daughter's issue with dishonesty is because she struggles with anxiety and her communication skills. So much of my problem is overcommunicating because I want a different relationship with her than I had with my mom. Addressing those issues was a huge step in bringing peace to our relationship. It didn't mean we rewarded lying, but it did mean we gave her some additional opportunities to get it right and that I had to focus on giving her the space and time she needed to feel comfortable approaching her dad and me.

Having her learn how to communicate openly and honestly with others is something we're always working on with all our kids, and understanding why she struggles with it has been eye-opening.

HEALING TAKES TIME AND EFFORT

One day, as we baked cookies for the holidays, I realized the relationship with my daughter didn't hurt anymore. It felt warm and fuzzy, like my favorite pair of soft wool socks.

We healed the blister by taking away the friction.

Here is the absolute truth: some preteens and teens are just harder than others. Some act out because they are frustrated, hurt, or confused, and their reaction is to lash out at someone they love. Some are so desperate for independence that they only know how to argue and painfully kick you away. Some are so hardheaded that they must learn things on their own, no matter how many times you tell them. Some struggle with issues such as people-pleasing, anxiety, communication, self-esteem, social skills, or a plethora of other traits that develop over time.

Or, like the situation with my daughter and me when we traveled through middle school, they are going through a tough time. As a parent, you might be going through a tough time, too.

You can fight it with all your might, but know that friction often causes blisters, and some can take a long time to heal.

Or you can take the friction away.

This is one of the hardest stories to tell because I am embarrassed by my behavior. My daughter's actions triggered all my shortcomings: my temper, my ego, and my inability to resolve conflict effectively.

But it also is a tale of triumph and growth and a shining example of how we can heal by working on ourselves.

I would be lying if I told you that my daughter and I had a perfect relationship after middle school. The truth is we still have a lot of ups and downs, but we never give up. I learned always to remember to see the best in her even when she showed us her worst, and she always forgave me when I let my emotions spin out of control.

I believe it's important to let you know how this story played out in the instance you're in a rough place with your child. While writing this book, I visited my daughter during her freshman year of college, now a student-athlete studying biology and genetics. Her roommate told me she is wonderful to live with and although she's not the neatest, she keeps her stuff on her half of the room. Her coach says she works hard, and her friends are warm and loving.

The best part? When we spend time together, we laugh, we share stories, and we enjoy each other's company. She still doesn't always listen to my advice, even when she asks for it; she still doesn't come to me immediately when there's a problem; and she still needs to learn things the hard way.

But I've learned to be patient, knowing that even though she's no longer in seventh grade, my daughter does things on her own time and in her own way.

During that college visit, my daughter and I discussed a tough moment she experienced in high school. She explained, "I know you tried to tell me, but I wasn't ready to hear it yet. I had to figure it out on my own."

I nodded my head because I get it. We have that in common.

And now we both know how to avoid blisters, a lesson we can take with us wherever we go.

MOVING FORWARD

Here are a few tips and tricks to make middle school a little easier. They might not solve everything, but you can learn from my mistakes!

- **Remember those awkward years.** One thing I forgot about the middle school years was just how uncomfortable I felt. I was uncomfortable in my new changing body, uncomfortable with acne, uncomfortable around my friends who seemed to get the social scene better than I did, and uncomfortable around the opposite sex. I felt uncomfortable talking about how uncomfortable and awkward I felt all the time. Our tweens and young teens have various responses during these years because they are trying to figure it all out. Plus, they have the added burden of social media and the Internet. It's a complicated time for our kids. Digging deep and leading with compassion can help.
- **Be flexible.** Middle school is a time when many parents start setting different rules for their kids. Some parents will provide their child with a cell phone and unfettered Internet and social media access; others will wait until much later. Some young tweens may be responsible enough to stay at home alone, and others do not yet have the

maturity to do so. Some middle schoolers will be allowed the freedom to go certain places on their own or date, while others will have no interest, or their parents will say no.

Each family deserves the opportunity to set their own rules and boundaries that they deem appropriate, but we should keep in mind that there will be times when it has social consequences for your child. For example, my daughters were left out of many social outings in middle school because they did not have Instagram yet. We had to get creative to solve it, but it was a fact of their life at the time. Another daughter's friend often stayed home by herself after school because her parents worked. While I certainly didn't mind them occasionally hanging out at her house, I encouraged them to come to ours because I worked from home and could be around more regularly.

You don't have to accommodate every ask, but if you feel your tween/young teen is responsible, it is okay for you to modify your rules depending on the situation. It's also a great time to teach about consequences and how they can earn responsibility over time.

- **Step back.** Middle school is a great time to start letting your child become more independent—even if they stumble. The natural consequences they may experience will not hurt them in the long term, as their teachers, coaches, leaders, and the like know that these skills, such as organization, time management, independent learning, and so on, are developing. This means that while your tweens and young teens may need some guidance on staying organized, it's also a good time to let them face uncomfortable outcomes when they forget a book, sports equipment, or lunch money. Give them the opportunity to figure it out and deal with the authority figure. Getting a stern lecture from a coach they respect or a zero on an assignment won't change your child's future, but not understanding the value of personal responsibility might.

- **Get to know the new them.** Middle school often brings new interests, people, and activities that may alter and shape your child in new ways. While you may have listened for hours about Minecraft or various YouTube videos, middle school is a great time to connect to what else may fuel your adolescent. Investing time to understand what your child loves is a great way to stay connected and (hopefully) get them to open up to you. Use whatever time you have to ask open-ended questions about what lights up their eyes. For example, it may be, "Tell me what you love about your history teacher," or "Tell me the rules of volleyball so I can follow the games better," or even "Will you teach me how to play your favorite video game?"

  As I mentioned, this is a time when middle schoolers may feel incredibly uncomfortable, even around dear old Mom and Dad, so whatever you can do to keep tabs and show how you are available to them can help pave the way for when they need to come to you for something important.

- **Parent the kid in front of you.** *We can't ignore what our kids need today because we fear they may miss out on something tomorrow.* If you think your child needs some downtime, give them that time. If you think they're too stressed at school, look at their schedule and adjust it. If you feel they need to speak to a therapist about an issue or to strengthen their mental health, do it. Don't worry so much about the future that you are willing to sacrifice their today.

  The healthiest young adults I know were often not at the top of their class, Division One athletes, or involved in every activity. Instead, they had time to pursue their passions, learned to build resilience through failure and natural consequences, and understood how to mitigate stress. Raising kids who understand their needs and how to care for them is a gift we give to the world.

- **Have fun.** While it's natural for middle schoolers to start to act more mature and disinterested in things they loved when they were younger, this shouldn't mean we stop having fun and being silly with them. Not every middle schooler can handle a parent who goes out of their way to embarrass them, but that shouldn't stop us from learning a TikTok dance, playing board games, or having a fun one-on-one date with them. And if you do the running man as good as I do, your kids may even be impressed!

CHAPTER FOUR

I WANT TO RAISE MORE THAN GOOD-ON-PAPER KIDS

Fill your paper with the breathings of your heart.
–William Wordsworth, English romantic poet

Right after I graduated college, I worked in Washington, DC, for a United States congressman. The staff was young and unmarried, and we spent most of our free time together after hours, going from receptions and cocktail parties to bars and social gatherings. Working in politics in our nation's capital was my dream job, but at the tender age of 22, I was the youngest with much to learn.

One morning, while we were all getting our coffee and about to start the workday, my colleague Liz told me about a date she went on the night before. Liz had just turned 30, so I thought she was worldly and had all the answers. I looked up to her as a professional mentor and as someone willing to teach me the lay of the land.

Liz had been very excited to go out to dinner with a staffer from another office, but it ended up a lackluster evening. She thought they had a lot in common, but it turned out there was no chemistry. She even mentioned that he was duller and a bit more pretentious than she thought he would be.

She explained, "I want to like him because he's so good on paper, but it didn't feel right."

I later found out that her date literally did look good on paper. He was a graduate of a prestigious law school, a frequent guest on television, and an up-and-coming staff member for a major player in Congress, but when it came to romance with my friend, it was a bust.

I've thought about that innocuous comment a thousand times since my conversation with Liz more than two decades ago. It reminds me that no matter the achievements I acquire on paper, what's more important is who I am as a person and the connection I can share with someone else.

And as much as this applies to who I want to be as a human being, it also applies to how we raise our kids in this achievement-based culture.

BUILDING UP HEARTS MORE THAN RESUMES

If you want to learn about what's happening in the world of teens and tweens, offer to drive carpool.

One weekday evening, I drove a gaggle of young teen girls to a soccer game. They started chitchatting after finding the right Spotify station and taking a few Snaps for their feeds. They went to four different high schools but seemed to tell the same stories.

However, I was unprepared for how disheartening, painful, and sad the commentary the girls shared about their fellow students would be.

There was a girl whose parents took her out of school because she suffered crippling anxiety about her grades. Anxiety and perfectionism consumed her, and she fought an eating disorder. There was a future Division One athlete who was a bully to other students (I think the exact quote was, "He is so douchey"). There was a middle school student who started a fake social media account to make fun of his peers. There was the story of a brother of one of the girls whose mental health was so bad that he needed to come home from college.

And they all had a story about a fellow student who dealt with suicidal ideation or died by suicide.

I wasn't entirely surprised to hear these stories about the classmates of my daughter and her friends. Unless you've been living under a rock, it's clear that adolescents today struggle with the stresses and pressures of today's chaotic world.

But something else nagged at me. These troubled kids all shared a common thread. They were stellar students, competitive athletes, school leaders, and high achievers. They won awards, volunteered at all the events, and highlighted their wins on social media with smiling faces and heart emojis.

They looked great on paper, but the state of their mental health and actions told another story.

These kids were all suffering, facing challenges, or hurting others, and because they appeared highly functioning and highly successful, their problems often were overshadowed by their achievements.

PERFORMANCE-BASED PARENTING IS KILLING OUR KIDS

In my discussions with parents, both in my everyday life and online as a parenting writer, I see that one of the things we all struggle with in raising adolescents is finding the balance in teaching our kids to push themselves to meet their potential without burning out or breaking down. We want our kids to learn how to work hard, meet goals, be productive—and make us proud.

But I noticed something when my teens started gearing up for high school. It's not enough to be merely good at something anymore, and average is irrelevant. For many, success is getting on the best team, having the highest GPA, or taking the most AP or dual-credit classes. It's going the farthest in your activity, winning the most awards, or getting selected for the most prestigious programs. And for many, it's doing all these things to gain acceptance into highly selective colleges.

The goalposts for success keep getting pushed further and further back, so far that I can't even see what success looks like anymore for kids.

For example, I noticed in the last few years that many of my friends who have teens who play extremely competitive soccer do not end up playing post–high school. Even though they have spent a lot of time and money attending college showcases, participating in tournaments, and utilizing personal trainers, most kids I know elected not to play their sport in college.

When I brought this up to some parents, they all had the same reaction: "They're just pretty burned out and want to focus on being a student for once."

I found this small sample interesting, so I cast a wider net. During a Thanksgiving break, I ran into a group of college students who were home and assembled at my friend's house. I asked a few about how high school academics differed from college. I was surprised when many shared that while the material was more difficult at their university, the pressure wasn't as intense. One boy even said, "For the first time, I feel like the goal is to learn the material instead of earning an A."

I posted a similar question in a parenting group I manage on Facebook. I asked, "If your student was super-involved in something in high school, do they pursue it with the same time commitment in college?"

The response was an overwhelming no. While many parents explained that their child might still play a sport via an intramural or club program, sing in a church choir, or volunteer, most said their kids seamlessly dropped something that defined them in high school.

Many respondents told me that their students often found something to fill their time that was fun. For example, the mom of a football player said her son joined an ultimate frisbee club, and a competitive cheer athlete discovered she had a passion for cartoons and animation. Others joined social clubs, political or interest groups, professional organizations, or something just for fun, such as the hammocking club (yes, that's a real thing on several college campuses).

These parents also conveyed that while they thought their teens' high school experiences were worthwhile, they wished they did some things differently. Instead of acting like that activity or sport was their entire life, they could have pursued other interests and hobbies, or maybe just had a few more hours of free time.

I believe this is the problem with focusing on defining success around performance instead of what you gain from the experience. Unfortunately, when success is only defined as something related to an achievement, success starts to feel limited. And when success feels limited, we start making crazy decisions to give our kids the best shot at being successful.

That may mean hiring incredibly expensive tutors and consultants to get our teens into top colleges or joining competitive sports teams that are miles away from our homes (guilty). It may mean ignoring our kids' mental health or comments that they want to quit an activity. It may mean calling a teacher about a bad grade or talking to a coach about playing time instead of letting your kid handle it.

It may even mean you secretly hope another child fails, so yours has the opportunity to try to succeed—not because you are mean-spirited, but instead just desperate for your kid to have the chance to shine.

Even when parents are on the same team or their kids are not competing against each other, rarely do they share information that could help others. We will do anything to give our kids an edge in their performance.

When we overly invest in our kids' achievements, we expect a return on investment for the time and money we spend on their behalf. We expect 100 percent effort every single time, no matter what, because it's not about what they learn while participating but about achievement.

But when we fill our adolescents' time with only these types of activities, they have no time or space to develop other parts of themselves, areas that may help them learn how to quiet their minds, cope with stress, or work with others. And when we interfere to help them achieve, they miss the opportunity to build grit and develop the resilience to overcome challenges.

This constant quest to push our kids to be their best, for perfection, for achieving, causes us to overschedule, over-push, and over-interfere so much that it often stresses out even the most capable kids.

You may not see it on their resumes, social media platforms, or even in their smiling personas—but anxiety, stress, and burnout are causing many of our brightest lights to dim.

When I went to my twin daughters' high school orientation, I remember their school principal standing up on stage encouraging parents to embrace the experience our kids could have over the next four years instead of focusing only on what may happen in the four years after. He encouraged us to avoid getting caught up in focusing on AP classes, varsity sports, and a whirlwind schedule that didn't allow students to take a breath.

I remember shuddering when he shared that more than one-fifth of all students were seeking some form of support for anxiety and depression (pre-pandemic), and we needed to address that by what we prioritized for our kids.

Moreover, that statement was personal to him. He shared a story about how his own son, who attended the same school where he was principal, was cut from the baseball team his sophomore year after spending so much time in a travel program (can you imagine how hard that must have been for the coach?).

Instead of using his pull as an administrator, he encouraged his son to get involved in just one other activity to fill his time. The young man joined our school's successful show choir, which spurred him to pursue a degree in music education. It was not the path his dad envisioned for his son, but it was the one that pointed him in the direction of happiness and fulfillment.

I am not saying your child pursuing an activity with relentless passion and focus is terrible. There is nothing wrong with achievement, winning, working hard, or dedicating yourself to a goal.

But as parents, we must recognize that achievement can become like an addiction for many people, and some teens can feel that if they aren't achieving, performing, or succeeding, then they are unlovable. It can leave these young people trying to figure out who they are in this world feeling empty, depressed, anxious, and perpetually unsatisfied.

It also puts an enormous and unnecessary strain on the relationship with our adolescent children. Because we spend so much of our time and resources on these activities, we want them to act like professionals and take it seriously. It's an unrealistic expectation for many kids at this age.

We must keep our eyes and hearts open to their wants, needs, and actions. We must listen to both the words they say and the actions we see. We must not inadvertently convey that what our kids achieve is who they are—which sometimes signals they aren't enough as is.

We must focus on the end goal: to raise productive adults who know how to handle and persevere through the bumps in the road of life.

And we must always remember that there is more than one path to success for our kids. We need to keep in mind that overcoming failure is a great tool for success in life. We must value heart and soul just as much as leadership and winning.

HOW DO WE STOP PERFORMANCE-BASED PARENTING?

So why are we overly invested in our children's performance? Why do we value results over experience? Why do we judge our parenting based on our children's achievements instead of their actions, experience, and joy in doing something they love?

I feel like these questions take a lot of self-examination to address effectively, which many of us are not equipped to do on our own.

I get it. I have had to fight these feelings myself. I often have to remind myself that what my child achieves has nothing to do with who I am as a person—and it isn't who they are, either.

But many of us are addicted to parenting validation. Like junkies, many parents are obsessed with engineering every aspect of their kids' lives to curate an unsustainable image. The need for affirmation about our parenting causes us to make irrational decisions and set standards for our kids that can only be achieved by an elite few.

Something to consider: if we want to give our kids a chance to become who they were meant to be, we need to let them direct their destiny.

WHERE DO WE START?

It can be a challenge for parents to take a step back at a time when we are trying to set up our kids for their futures. Think of it like teaching your child to ride a bike. You are staying close in case they fall, but they are steering and learning how to take control. Here are some thoughts to get you started:

- **Get out of their way.** We need to stop micromanaging their lives and trying to fill every time void with lessons, enrichment, and skill development. We need to give them space to figure out what they enjoy doing as opposed to only doing what we expect of them. And we need to listen and look for cues that they may be experiencing burnout, stress, or a breakdown. Their mental health always needs to come first.

- **Remember their age.** Have you ever been on the sidelines of youth sports when you hear an aggressive parent shouting at their kids? Or have you ever inadvertently overheard a parent tearing into their child for a grade, bad performance, or mistake? It's the worst when you see it, yet so many of us do it.

  There is a difference between accountability and encouragement and beratement and bullying. We need to treat our adolescents at their age level instead of like professionals or mini-adults. The focus should be on fun, learning, experience, and creativity instead of positioning them solely for a future they may not even want in a few years. Listen to them if they want to take time away from a sport or activity, but more importantly, talk to them about why they might need a break. Remember that sometimes it can be a positive to step away, gain perspective, and focus on something else for some time. We can't ignore the signs of what they need *today* for what they may miss out on in the future.

- **Stay connected.** When our teens do find a passion and go all-in, we still need to monitor their mental health and well-being. Some kids do not have an off switch, and it's our job as parents to remind them to put self-care first—and that it's okay to miss one meeting, practice, or game when you feel yourself deteriorating. It's even more important to model this for them. There must be a balance between responsibility to a team or group and responsibility for self.

- **Remember what the teen years are for.** Growing up is a process, not an event. That means we cannot let our fears and anxieties get in the way of what our kids may learn from their choices. Adolescence is a time for discovery, experimenting, and taking healthy risks to figure out who you are. While you may think your daughter is giving up a potential professional dancing career, she may only want to experience a typical life as a teenager. Or if your son wants to be a freelance photographer instead of a student at a competitive college, that does not mean you failed as a parent. If we desire a long-term relationship with our kids, we need to listen to them today.

- **Where you go to college is not who you are.** Journalist Frank Bruni wrote a manifesto back in 2016 entitled *Where You Go Is Not Who You'll Be* to address the hype around college admissions and the race to get an acceptance to "elite" colleges. Unfortunately, the college admissions process is still out of control, and many students and their parents spend an inordinate amount of time and resources trying to build up resumes that fit a mold of what's perceived as a desirable candidate for a college. This is a major reason why many students arrive at campus stressed and burned out.

  As parents, we have to remind our kids that working hard and finding your passion will set them up for a successful life more than doing it simply to gain admission to a certain school. I try to tell the teens in my life that test scores, grades, and activities may give them more choices, but it does not mean they can't pursue their passion.

I understand that this is easier said than done. Sometimes, it feels like we make these decisions while staring down the barrel of a shotgun. Sometimes, it feels lonely, isolating, and overwhelming.

I get it and I've been there. It's scary. And when you try to take a step back and find some balance, the rest of the world does not make it easy to make these decisions.

Sometimes, you have to fight with your child's school to create a more grade-level-appropriate schedule or deal with well-meaning family members whose unending comments about how sad it is that your son quit piano make you question your decision. Club sports coaches will try to convince you to invest more time on skill development, and instructors will often upsell you on lessons.

There are times when aggressively pursuing a dream is exactly what your child wants, but not everything in their life needs to be rigorous or challenging. We can't put 100 percent into everything we do. It's not healthy, nor is it productive.

It's okay to do something for fun, to learn, or simply to relax. We should pressure our communities to focus on providing these opportunities to our kids, like art, music, and recreational sports, since these often disappear during the teen years.

And we must remind ourselves (over and over again) that success for our kids is not limited, and there is not one way to be successful. That means your choices for your family are specific to your unique situation and values, not dependent on what anyone else deems important.

HOW DO WE FIND THE BALANCE WHEN RAISING OUR TEENS?

We all want our kids to build a strong work ethic, understand personal responsibility, and be motivated to change and grow, but we have to fill up their hearts as much as their resumes.

Focusing on the performance instead of the process creates the illusion of leaders, instead of teaching kids the skills to motivate others.

Often, we focus on increasing the numbers on their GPA and standardized test scores over gaining life skills and coping mechanisms. We want them to gain more placeholders on a college application instead of passions that can get our kids through dark times. We want more trophies, medals, and certificates than hobbies and downtime.

We want our kids to look good to the rest of the world even though they often feel so anxious, depressed, and tired that they crumble when life feels too much—or worse, they lash out at others.

Sometimes, we forget that parenting is a long game. We need to play chess, not checkers.

We must make tough choices that are in the best interests of our families and be willing to live with the unknown consequences. We might choose sports clubs that reduce driving time or a class schedule that allows the pursuit of a passion project. We might allow our teens to take a more manageable schedule to protect their mental health, knowing it may limit their college choices. We might encourage them to participate in activities on a more recreational basis so they can protect their free time.

And yes, your kids may not look as strong on paper as other kids, but you may raise healthier, more well-rounded adults who know how to manage their emotions in a complex world. You might have kids who are less stressed, less anxious, and more optimistic and who are good life partners. They may have hobbies that keep them from feeling lonely and isolated or start building experience toward a fulfilling life career.

My end goal is to send kids out into this world who are happy, who know how to cope, and who know how to care for themselves and others when life gets tough.

I have never seen a line for that on a resume.

Of course, you can have both. You can help your child assemble an impressive list of accomplishments and raise a well-adjusted adult.

But I believe as parents, we can't lose sight of what we really want for our children—a peaceful mind, joy in their hearts, and people who love them. You can't hang those on a wall or brag about them on social media, but it can determine how they feel about themselves and others.

That starts with taking a holistic look at your child and committing to making tough choices for them today that will pay off in the long run.

I don't want to raise good-on-paper kids. I want my children to be as impressive in living color as any words you can read about them on a white sheet.

MOVING FORWARD

- **Remain flexible.** Remind yourself that many successful adults have fluid careers and interests, so allowing your teen to try out different activities does not make them flaky. Instead, it's an opportunity for them to discover their likes and dislikes.
- **Know the "why."** Whether your child wants to quit an activity or pursue something new, find out their "why." Do they want to quit because they no longer enjoy it or because they have a problem with a coach? Do they want to try an activity because their friends are in it or because they think it will help them get into college? Their answers aren't wrong, but you can guide them better if you let them take the lead.
- **Remember your role.** Without a doubt, parents have the greatest impact on a child's character. Do you want to be an encourager or a drill sergeant? Do you want to be a taxi driver or a trusted confidant? As parents and caregivers we have the opportunity to shape how our kids will approach problems, solve conflicts, and maintain relationships. We should focus on building up those skills more than building up their resume.

CHAPTER FIVE

WHOSE DREAM IS IT?

We grow great by dreams.
  –Woodrow Wilson, 28th president of the United States

"Three girls so close together! Wow, you'll have your hands full."

If only I had a quarter for every time I heard those words over the past 18 years, I'd be a multimillionaire.

It was the same sentiment for my husband, except many people often tacked on another observation: "Wow. Three girls? You're screwed. Are you going to try for a son?"

And my spouse would laughingly joke, "Well, I wanted to take one out for a test drive, and we ended up with three in sixteen months, so I'm going to say I'm pretty happy with what I got." Then he would add, "I just hope one of them plays soccer."

WE ALL HAVE DREAMS FOR OUR CHILDREN

When the nurse puts that new baby in your arms, it's hard not to imagine a life full of promise and potential for them. You might picture them graduating at the top of their class and attending a prestigious university. You might see them winning an Olympic gold medal in your favorite sport. You visualize your daughter winning a presidential election or your son finding the cure for cancer.

The possibilities for your child seem endless because they are.

When they're little, everything your child does seems amazing. Their first steps, their first words, the first time they name a color or memorize a song. We revel in these successes because they are their own and not in comparison to anyone else's.

Every child is gifted. Every child has enormous potential.

As they age, we start seeing glimmers of who they could be. We see our three-year-olds confidently up on stage and then start believing they could win a Tony award for best lead in a musical. When our preschoolers show an aptitude toward reading, people tell us it is a sign of profound intellectual ability, so you start saving for Harvard. Watching your five-year-old swim across the family pool, you may think you're raising the next Michael Phelps. When your son memorizes the name of every dinosaur, you can't help but believe their destiny is to lead the world in science and discovery.

The future is unlimited when they're young, and they take the lead with their interests and time.

What parent does not want the best for their child? Our job is to have an unconditional and unwavering belief in our kids. If we don't believe they can reach the stars, then who will? If we won't be their soft place to land when they fall or burn out, then who will?

But sometimes we confuse wanting the best *for them* with expecting them to be the best in whatever they pursue. One is about *them*; the other is about *us*.

When we unintentionally put too much stock into the dreams we have for our kids, it can end up fracturing the relationship, particularly during the volatile tween and teen years when kids start voicing their opinions more frequently and figuring out where and how they want to spend their time.

We tell our children they should "dream big" and "reach for the stars," but our words and actions don't always align. What we're actually saying between the lines is "I know what your dream should be," or "I believe in you, as long as you do what I think is best."

Sometimes we're so invested in "their dream" that we push them to do more, even when they show signs of fatigue or burnout. We discourage them from quitting because we fear they're throwing away an opportunity. We pursue activities for trophies, accolades, and lines on a resume instead of for pleasure and life lessons. We act disappointed at their performance and tell them when we don't think they're trying hard enough or meeting their potential. We guide them toward a certain path because we want them to avoid making the same mistakes we did at their age. We put their activities as priorities over everything, including school, family time, self-care, and sleep.

You don't have to look too deep into our culture to see how a parent's and child's dreams can intertwine. Some examples are troubling, like soccer player Gio Reyna, whose disgruntled parents interfered with their son's place on the US national soccer team, or how Britney Spears's father abused his daughter's fame and wealth through a misguided conservatorship. These parents used the guise of their child's abilities to pursue their own personal interests. Sometimes it's commendable and uncomfortable, like Venus and Serena Williams's father, whose laser focus and unrelenting dedication built a tennis empire.

But you also see it in our hometowns, such as the family willing to go into debt to pay for competitive dance programs, the dad who yells at a teenage referee because they made a bad call, or the mom who calls a teacher to get a grade changed so their child can get into a specific type of college.

What looks like love and support for a child can sometimes mask insecurity, fear, greed, and in some extreme circumstances, borderline abuse.

I believe the hopes and dreams we have for our kids always stem from a place of love, but sometimes we want our kids' successes and achievements to fill in the cracks we have within ourselves. We unintentionally use our kids to curb our disappointment for dreams we had to defer, or we may use them to build up our self-esteem that has taken blows over the years. We may even piggyback on our children's successes to bring joy to an unfulfilling or mundane life.

It's tough to know when you cross over to the dark side. It's a thin line between being a supportive parent and a Tiger Mom, and the reasons can be deeply rooted in our past, often a place we don't want to return to explore. And some parents look at their children as a second chance to get their dreams right.

Modern parents also feel intense pressure to give their kids—especially their adolescent children who will launch into the world soon—advantages that offer the best chance at a great life. "Keeping up with the Joneses" takes on a new level as social media often fuels this pressure to conform to a completely unrealistic and unachievable ideal of what a "good" parent looks like.

The problem arises when parents transfer their baggage to their offspring and try to get their needs met or dreams achieved by living vicariously through their kids; it puts tremendous pressure on a tween or teen who may already feel overwhelmed by the everyday pressures of adolescence and the chaotic world around them.

Here is a hard truth. When you try to fill a void in yourself through your kids' achievements, you're robbing them of their ability to discover their passions, talents, interests, and perhaps even a future career. It is also possible that your child starts to feel like your love is conditional based on achieving your dreams, goals, and desires, as opposed to who your child is now.

For most people, this can be a challenging self-analysis (speaking from some experience). It can be tough to identify unless you're looking for it.

Some questions you can ask yourself include:

- *Are you pushing your child toward something because they have expressed an interest, or because you think it's what's best for them?*
- *Do you chastise your child for their effort and dedication, or do you measure success based on their enjoyment and attitude toward the activity?*
- *Do you feel like the stress of their activity interferes with your daily life or ability to control your emotions? (Tryout season used to be the worst in our house!)*
- *Do your past regrets constantly come up in discussions with your child, such as telling them that you felt quitting something was a huge mistake for you?*
- *Do you micromanage their time surrounding certain activities, such as reminding them about practicing, taking care of their preparation, talking about it at meals, and so on?*
- *Do you frequently talk to coaches/advisors/teachers about their decisions, argue about your child's placement, or belittle other parents or participants at home or with friends? Do you struggle with controlling your anger at events?*
- *Is your self-worth tied to your child's participation and achievements, such as feeling embarrassed by their performance or taking ownership of their achievements?*
- *Do you find yourself saying, "I wish someone had pushed me," or "I'm only saying this for your own good"?*
- *Do you ignore signs that your child isn't enjoying an activity, such as not wanting to practice, complaining about going, mood swings, or comments about quitting?*

While it may be tough to see yourself reflected in those questions, if you answered yes to one or more, you may need to reassess how you discuss your adolescent's schedule.

And before you start beating yourself up for it, please know that so many of us have been there, too. I've done many of these things myself, and I'm not proud of it. But what I am proud of is that I grew through it. Learning to separate my past from my kids' present helped me more than I can convey. Stepping back and letting them take ownership and accountability helped my daughters gain confidence and grow their self-esteem. And untethering their achievements from my self-worth as a parent brought a new foundation of peace to our relationship that freed us all to be our best selves (well, at least most of the time).

What if the most productive thing we can do for our tweens and teens is step back instead of push? What if they need us more to sit with them quietly in their struggles as opposed to sitting in a car back and forth to practice? What if when they talked, we listened—and believed that they knew what was best for their own well-being? What if we let them start standing on their own two feet while under our roof so we know they can stand strong when they're out in the world alone?

What if we believed in them so much that they started to believe in themselves?

WHEN WE LOSE OUR WAY, WE CAN ALWAYS PIVOT

In my house, all three of my kids were in soccer gear by the age of four. They may have worn pink socks, pink cleats, and sparkly headbands, but they knew how to kick a ball before taking their first step.

It didn't take long to see one of our daughters was way more interested in picking dandelions on the field than entering a toddler scrum to fight over a ball, so she retired early. We were all in with the other two, however. And while their experience with the sport was mostly positive, there were times I also knew that my husband and I didn't have our heads on entirely straight.

Looking back on it now, it's easy to see, but when we were in the thick of it? It was, and at times we were, the worst. Like, why were soccer tryouts so dramatic that sometimes it impacted our sleep?

Why were we so disappointed when one of our daughters had a bad game? Or why were the relationships with other parents often so awkward?

While soccer dominated much of our time, I experienced this phenomenon in many other areas of my daughters' lives. I've heard many parents discuss it as well, whether it was academics, music, student government, scholastic endeavors, or even Scouts. Everything is competitive nowadays.

For many, letting our older children walk away from something in which they (and we) have invested a significant amount of time (and most likely money) during their short lives often feels like such a difficult decision, even when your child has lost the joy and purpose of those same activities.

FOMO in parenting is real. It equates to a feeling of fear that your child may be left behind if they miss one session, one practice, one event. The premise that if you don't declare your interest at an early age and invest in one thing, then you can't be successful, is hurting our kids.

It's causing today's teens and tweens to burn out and get depressed. It's causing them to stifle their interests and passions. It's causing them to become bitter and resentful.

And it's ruining our relationships with them.

Our goal should be for our kids to learn life lessons from their extracurricular activities, such as leadership, teamwork, grit, and perseverance. We should want our kids to find healthy hobbies and pursuits that fill them up so that when they struggle in life, they have something to turn to that brings them joy. Kids should be able to try different activities to become well-rounded individuals instead of pawns to fill our personal voids and cash cows that fill someone else's pockets.

And they should know that it's okay for *their* dreams, *their* interests, *and their* passions to change. We must be willing to let go of any preconceived paths we want them to walk so they can discover what lights them up.

When one of my daughters decided to quit soccer during her freshman year of high school, it felt odd that it was such a big deal to so many people. She had kicked a black-and-white ball since she could place one foot after the other, but she hadn't enjoyed it for a few years.

We've always told her to dream big, have goals, and work hard. And she did that.

She and her dad always talked about having a shared experience of playing on a competitive high school team one day. She often traded sleepovers for early morning games and played in the freezing rain while her friends sat warmly in movie theaters or shopping malls—never once complaining.

But we could see her struggling. We could see her enthusiasm draining both on and off the field. And we sensed that she was worried about disappointing us.

In eighth grade, she decided on a whim to run cross-country and track for her middle school while still playing club soccer. It was a lot on her and on us, but we could see her coming to life in her new sport.

My husband and I were the ones to bring it up to her. We said the words first: "It's okay if you want to quit soccer."

But she wasn't ready yet. She knew she had invested much time, effort, and money in a sport she loved and believed she would always play. Deep down, I also think she worried about what her dad felt about it.

But by that time in her young life, when we knew she was in a place that did not bring her joy, we didn't see it the way she thought we did. While I brought it up to her several times, a conversation with her dad finally helped her drop the hammer. Her small face relaxed when her father said, "I'll miss watching you on the pitch, but what I really want to see is you doing what you love."

We told her it's okay for dreams to change—hers and ours. Every step she took playing soccer led her somewhere else, maybe even someplace better. Her dad wanted the sport to bring her the same joy and positive experience that it brought him as a high school and Division Three athlete, but he recognized that she could get those life lessons through many different avenues.

She ran cross-country and played soccer for one more year, but it was incredibly tough on her body. At the end of the season, she meekly said, "I think I'm done playing soccer and want to focus on running."

And that she did.

For her, quitting led to a spot on a D3 cross-country and track team for college, an opportunity she might not have had if she continued playing soccer. And, as a family, we fell in love with a new sport solely because she loved it first.

My youngest daughter still plays, and it is her favorite pastime. For a few years she was also a team member at a competitive club that often traveled out of state, and practices were up to 45 minutes away. Her team had a challenging year, and although she still loved the sport, we could tell she wasn't enjoying it like she had in years past.

After many discussions, we asked her if she would like to return to our local town club so she could play with her friends, and it was closer to home. At first she wasn't sure, but after thinking about it, she became more excited. We made the switch, and she never looked back.

After two seasons, the club owner approached my daughter to see if she would like to help coach a team of fourth-grade girls. Wanting to become an educator, my daughter leaped at the opportunity.

When you talk to her now, she would say that coaching is her passion. She spends her time mentoring younger players, teaching them tricks, and serving as a role model. It is her favorite part of her soccer experience, and while I believe she is an excellent coach and player, leading these young girls has boosted her confidence and self-esteem. As a parent, it is exactly what you want your child to get out of sports.

I don't believe she would have had this opportunity if we stayed at her former club, where we spent more time and money than she was getting out of it. The most enriching experience for her did not come from pursuing the most competitive option; it came from choosing the best option for her health and well-being.

And my daughter who spent her short soccer experience picking flowers? She is an accomplished cellist who also joined the marching band her senior year as a member of the Color Guard, ran cross-country for a season, learned to ride horses, joined her high school literary magazine, and played in the pit orchestra for her high school's musical.

At first, it was tough to embrace these activities we knew nothing about, but by the end of each season, we were learning to cheer as loud (or louder) for a successful flag toss as we had for a soccer goal. Sometimes we were disappointed when she decided no longer to pursue something we grew to enjoy, but watching her confidently try new things was a gift.

It takes courage for our kids to give up something they've poured their heart and soul into to pursue something different, just as it takes courage for any tween or teen to try something new.

But it also takes courage for a parent to step back and recognize that what's best for our kids may not be what we want for them; it's the dream they want to chase for themselves. We need to have faith that our child can figure it out no matter what the choices are.

Most of all, it takes an unrelenting belief that listening to what our tweens' and teens' needs are today provides the best opportunity for them to be surefooted tomorrow. Our big kids should never feel obliged to keep doing something for fear of disappointing those who are supposed to love them unconditionally, and we should not force them to do something because of our own fears, insecurities, or unfulfilled hopes and desires.

Their performance should never be tied to our self-worth. Their achievements shouldn't determine what we put on our social media feeds. Their dreams should never make them feel stuck, never be carried like a burden, never make them feel like a prisoner, and never feel conditional to our love.

Dreams should fuel our ambition, fire our passion, and help us learn about ourselves.

As parents, our dreams for them shouldn't define our kids. Their dreams shouldn't define them either. Instead, dreams can help us figure out who we want to become.

We don't want our growing kids to give up on something because it's hard or they aren't good at it. We don't want them to quit because someone said it was silly or not worth doing.

Instead, we should encourage our kids to pursue their dreams with gusto, but it's okay if they change direction. It's okay to try something new. It's okay to take a break and rest.

It's okay to give up on a dream because you've replaced it with a different one.

Our job as parents is always to be rooting for our kids. Our unconditional love can never waver, even when we don't understand it. We want our kids to know they can go big but can always come home to dream again.

MOVING FORWARD

Are you concerned that your tween or teen is stuck in an activity, overscheduled, or pursuing something for a parent as opposed to for themselves? Here are a few ways to approach the subject:

- If your child spends a significant amount of time solely on one activity, talk to them about finding an unrelated hobby they can pursue in their downtime without ties to the activity.
- Do regular check-ins to see how they're feeling about their schedule. Give them permission to quit if you see signs that they're unhappy.
- Encourage scheduling blocks of time where they can do something creative.
- Model having a hobby or something you pursue for fun or leisure. Ask your teen to join you.
- Point out their talents. If they bake something delicious, encourage them to do more. Acknowledge their artistic abilities if they usually focus on athletics. Notice if they enjoy taking photos or videos. Find out if they're good at video games, which often require strategic thinking and strong hand-eye coordination. Encourage them to exercise in different ways.
- Cheer for character attributes about your kids, not their activities or accomplishments (Joey is a great teammate rather than saying a great volleyball player; Jody has a great work ethic, as opposed to being the top violinist).
- Discuss the importance of self-care—physically, mentally, and spiritually. Encourage your kids to take time out to focus on nourishing their brains, body, and spirit.
- Stay in tune with your own emotions. Ensure that your child understands your love for them is not dependent upon what activities they do.
- Be thoughtful about what you post on social media.

CHAPTER SIX

SOFT PARENTING IN A HARD WORLD

Water is fluid, soft, and yielding. But water will wear away rock, which is rigid and cannot yield. As a rule, whatever is fluid, soft, and yielding will overcome whatever is rigid and hard. This is another paradox: what is soft is strong.

—Lao Tzu, Chinese philosopher

One Saturday afternoon when I was in high school, I remember my mother losing her mind because I had not yet put away my shoes.

We lived on the Gulf Coast side of Florida, and as usual, I spent most of the day at the beach with my friends. As I often did, I cut it close to make it to my part-time job as a waitress in a retirement facility. As I strolled through our front door, I casually shouted, "Hi, it's me! I'm just grabbing my stuff, and then I'm headed to work."

As I breezily walked down the hallway toward my room without a care in the world, I felt a whisk of air as something white flew past my head and then was startled as something hit me in my backside. I whirled around to see my mom standing 15 feet away, hurling shoe after shoe at me, including my white leather Sam & Libby flats, a black pair of shoes I wore to work, my gym sneakers for school, and a pair of flip-flops.

"I told you not to leave the house without putting these away," she bellowed. After that, I think I blacked out because my mom was scary. She didn't weigh much more than a hundred pounds, but I always, always, maintained a healthy dose of fear of her.

That healthy dose of fear ensured that I rarely talked back. I learned to do just enough to avoid my mother yelling at me. I learned that pleasing her was better than getting on her wrong side. I learned that when I did push limits, I was much more scared of my mom than I was of whatever risk I was participating in at the time.

I also learned to circumvent the truth. I would do anything to avoid my parents freaking out on me, and I learned a little white lie could prevent a big fight.

Now that I'm an adult, I understand why my mom is built of iron. She is a survivor who has endured everything that life has thrown at her. Don't get me wrong. My mom is a living, breathing saint, who is also warm, loving, and dedicated to my well-being, but she also scared the crap out of me growing up (she still does a little bit).

My mom grew up in a dilapidated farmhouse in Ohio in the 1940s and '50s. She was the oldest of eight children and didn't have much money or opportunity during that time. Based on the stories she shares about her youth, which included an absent father and a flighty mom, it's remarkable that she thrived and lived such a fruitful life.

She joined the Air Force immediately after high school graduation, met my dad in September, and was married by the end of the year. By 19 she had her first child and was learning to care for her new family.

My mom is the strongest, hardest-working person I know. She always held a part-time job to help pay for activities for me and my siblings, opened her home to relatives in need, and moved in with my family twice to help care for us when I was ill, first when on bedrest with my twins, and again when I faced a debilitating eye disease in my early 40s.

While my mom was the primary day-to-day parent, my dad was the wild card. An altar boy who grew up in the Bronx with a single mother, he dropped out of high school when he was 16. He hustled working jobs at his uncle's New York diner and driving cabs and enlisted first in the Navy and then later the Air Force, where he met my mom. He eventually earned his GED and worked his way up to become a regional sales director at a chemical company, and later started his own business.

Most days he was my biggest cheerleader, but he was also old school. If my brother and I were bickering, he would reach over and deliver such a flick to my ear that I would feel it for days. He would let me get away with breaking a house rule and then lose his temper because I dropped the ketchup cap. He would slip me a $10 bill just for fun and later make the house shake when he was angry.

By all accounts, the fact that my parents built a loving home and marriage despite their humble and troubled beginnings is an incredible accomplishment, and I know how lucky I was to be raised by them. They were the epitome of giving their children more than they ever had—emotionally, financially, and opportunistically. My parents weren't perfect. They didn't need to be. They provided me with so much more than they were ever given. They did not lament about their past, but instead changed their future.

And while I admire and love my parents so much, I also now understand I grew up in a house that lacked communication skills, skills I think I desperately needed to develop, skills that were never shown to them either.

I did not learn how to resolve conflict, because the expectation was to obey without question. I was embarrassed to talk about topics such as my period, sex, or dating because those were never mentioned. I often tried to circumvent my parents' rules instead of discussing them because they had a "my way or the highway" approach.

And while I was a teen from a loving and supporting home who was involved in school, a cheerleader, and a strong student, I struggled with friendships and with my first few serious relationships during my teen years and early adulthood.

I was a yeller when I was angry. I avoided addressing issues until I was really frustrated, or worse, brought them up after I was drinking. And I was embarrassed to talk about important, life-saving topics, such as sexual history or consent.

When I became a parent myself, I fell into the trap of overcommunicating. I so badly wanted my kids to come to me that I often pushed too hard, asked too many questions, and turned everything into a life lesson. It ended up doing the exact opposite of what I wanted.

I don't blame this on my parents. They grew up in a time when alcoholism was rampant, mental health was ignored, and feelings were muted. They did their best with what they had, and both continued to grow and learn as they aged, and I love that my mom and I can talk openly about our past and how I parent now.

But as I raise my teens in today's modern world, I want a different relationship than the one I had with my parents during those teen years. It's tough, however, to find the balance between the hard edge of authoritarian parenting and letting your emotional teenagers walk all over you.

THERE IS NO MANUAL FOR RAISING TODAY'S TEENAGERS

Do you ever notice on social media that people love to point out everything teens do wrong today? They say teens are lazy, entitled, and selfish. They claim that teens lack resilience, motivation, and direction.

Often this also goes hand in hand with knocking the parents for all the things they're doing wrong. But we never address the root issue: most of us were not raised with the skills to have healthy relationships.

It's not uncommon to hear of parents who say they're struggling with disrespectful behavior and backtalk from their teens, and most of us agree that we would never have spoken to our parents that way. My mom and dad would have knocked me into next Sunday if I said a few of the things my kids spewed to me over the years.

But the consequence of that fear was I didn't open up to them that much about the hard stuff. Discussions in my house often were disguised as threats. "I'll kill you if I catch you drinking and driving." Or "I swear to God if you get pregnant . . . ."

I never truly felt like I could come to them until I was much older and less scared they would ground me (so, probably in my mid-20s, when I could pay for myself).

I don't look back at my childhood in a negative way. In fact, I know that my parents instilled in me the foundation for a strong work ethic, resilience, empathy, and generosity that have served me well throughout my life.

But I also carried a burden with me into every relationship. I feared someone would shut me down or cut me out if I was honest or if I was too embarrassed and self-conscious to discuss a topic.

SOMETIMES LOVING THROUGH THE HARD MEANS GIVING GRACE

One night, I was deep in a comment section of a Facebook group where someone was discussing how their teen daughter stormed through their front door, threw her books down on the counter, told her mom to leave her alone, and stomped up to her room.

The mom was distraught. Her daughter typically didn't act that way, and she had no idea what to do next. She literally was typing comments from her phone while her daughter stewed on the other side of her bedroom door.

This diverse group offered varying pieces of advice. Many commenters stated that they would never accept this disrespect and the mom should make her daughter return downstairs to pick up her stuff. They would never allow this behavior in their house. There were a few people who called the girl overdramatic, blamed it on puberty hormones, or even implied that the mom was a pushover.

As I continued to scroll, I happened upon a comment so filled with compassion that it brought tears to my eyes. "I would pick up her stuff, bring a snack, and leave it by her door. Let her know you are there if she needs to talk. Volatile behavior is often caused by a storm that is brewing inside. You can be her soft place to land or another rock she needs to climb."

Oof. That got me in the feels. Because at the end of the day, that young girl probably had so much turmoil brewing inside of her that forcing her to clean up her mess at that moment might have broken her completely.

And who would that action be for—the girl or the parent?

SOFT DOES NOT MEAN YOU'RE A DOORMAT

I know many people who call me "soft." It usually rolls off me, but sometimes I get defensive because it feels like a cutting criticism of my parenting. As someone who is constantly trying to maintain control over her emotions and fights anxious thoughts, I sometimes find it hard to know where the line is for what is disrespectful behavior, what is typical teen angst, and what could be a call for help.

One evening, when our family of five had our regular Sunday night dinner, my daughter asked me in between bites of her hamburger if I was ever scared about getting roofied.

"When did that start, Mom?" she asked. "Did it happen when you were in college?"

I've always been incredibly open with my kids about things I encountered during my teenage years, so this was not out of the ordinary. But then the questions started coming like rapid-fire.

We talked about fraternity parties and watching some of my friends drink too much. I shared a troubling encounter with a date that left me unnerved for months. I took a deep breath and told them in detail about a scary experience I had with drugs during my sophomore year. I told them about a classmate who was sexually assaulted by someone she trusted.

We discussed the importance of the buddy system at parties and how I forced a few friends to come home with me even when they didn't want to. My husband shared tips on identifying someone who drank too much. We reminded them there was never a situation when they couldn't come to us and never a time when we wouldn't help.

They continued to ask, and I continued to answer, just as I have always done, just as I always will.

And that night I laid in my bed so incredibly thankful that my daughters were comfortable enough with me to ask questions, comfortable enough with me to share some of their own experiences.

True, I haven't always liked the way my daughters have talked to me in the past. There have been times when they were disrespectful or snotty or just cruel, times when words came out of their mouths that I never would have said to my parents.

But I also would never have come to my mom and dad to talk to them about drugs or alcohol. I would never have come to my parents to talk about sex or my fears or problems. I would never have come to them to talk about anything difficult or uncomfortable.

They were great parents, and I respected them, but with that fear came an unspoken level of distrust that meant I couldn't open up to them, that I couldn't quite be myself.

So there have been times I did not like the way they treated me. Perhaps I let a few things slide that I could have addressed differently. Yes, I sometimes wish they were a little fearful of me, just as I had been of my mom.

But knowing that my kids have come to me, opened up to me, and trusted me to be a place they could turn to when unsure about this world—well, I wouldn't trade that for anything.

Over the last few years, we've used the term "safe space" excessively when it comes to creating an environment where people can feel secure that they will not be exposed to discrimination, criticism, harassment, or any other emotional or physical harm. In parenting, a safe space is often about creating an environment where people can share their emotions without fear of judgment and, for most teenagers, without punishment.

That does not mean you're a doormat, or you don't have rules and boundaries, but it is that unconditional love thing we often say we have for our kids.

I always told my daughters they could come to me with anything, and we would talk it out first before discussing any consequences. I also told them they could start a conversation in whatever way they felt comfortable, whether a hand-written note, text message, or meme.

Becoming a "safe space" for your teens is a little bit of a tradeoff. You have to take the good with the bad, lose a little bit of power, and believe that not responding to every behavior will make your relationship stronger instead of your role as a parent weaker.

You have to learn to disengage to keep them engaged.

Knowing that my weak point was reacting emotionally when my adolescent children were emotional, I knew I needed to prepare myself with a toolbox of responses to diffuse a situation. Having some phrases ready for moments when we were teetering at the edge of a confrontation helped me tremendously. Here are some examples:

- "I know you're upset, but you can't talk to me that way. I'll be in my room if you'd like to discuss it," and then withhold the lecture.
- "I have listened to your side and now provided an answer. If you have new information, you can share it with me, otherwise this particular conversation is over."
- "I can tell you're stressed. I can help you get a few things done or stay out of your way. Let me know what you need right now."
- "Do you want my advice, or do you just want to vent? I'm cool with either."
- "Thank you for telling me. Can I take a few minutes to process this information before we discuss it further?"
- "I want to answer your question, but I need a minute to compose myself."

Or sometimes you can let some bad behavior slide by and ignore it. As someone once said, "You don't have to attend every argument you are invited to."

Being a soft parent means you also remain malleable. You have to set boundaries but be willing to move them. Enforce rules but be willing to change them depending on the circumstance. Offer grace, so much grace, for the chaotic issues our teens face today.

And sometimes it means letting them lash out and staying aware enough to know it's not you. They just have nowhere else to put that firestorm of emotions swirling inside them.

So, yes, I'm soft, and I'm raising soft kids.

I'm soft because I try to be more flexible in this complex world. I'm soft because I believe my kids are getting pushed and pressured from all directions, much more than I did growing up. I'm soft so that my kids know they can come to me about anything and get honest answers about tough issues.

Soft has made our relationship strong. Soft has made them self-confident. Soft has made them feel safe.

And if loving hard makes me soft, I'm okay with that.

MOVING FORWARD

- **Define what is important to *you* in regard to the relationship with your teen.** Understand that your relationship does not need to look the same as other families, or the same as it was between you and your parents. Once you understand what you want it to look like, you can start working toward that goal.
- **Set boundaries, but not in the heat of the moment.** As parents, we often try to set boundaries and issue consequences at the wrong times. We need to set boundaries, such as respectful communication, curfews, family house rules, or expectations of behavior when everyone is calm and not in the middle of stress or a meltdown. Be specific, and don't be afraid to write down rules and consequences so everyone agrees.

- **Remember that parenting is fluid.** While it's important to be specific with your teen about your rules and expectations, that does not mean you can't be flexible. While your teen is still tethered to you while living under your roof, you can always extend the rope out a little farther as your teen proves they are responsible and trustworthy, or pull it back as needed.

CHAPTER SEVEN

SOMETIMES WE HAVE TO LET THEM TRY STUFF ON

Find out who you are and do it on purpose.
–Dolly Parton, entertainer, author, entrepreneur, and activist

A seriously bad spiral perm defined a good chunk of my high school years. Well, it was one okay perm and one exceptionally bad spiral perm that could make a prize-winning poodle envious.

I have strengths, but fashion and beauty are not one of them. I have never been one to know how to do certain hair styles, put together a cool outfit, or paint my nails. It hasn't stopped me from trying, but I was never very good at it, and I have some painful late '80s and early '90s photos to prove it.

I asked for my first perm in ninth grade. It was basic and in line with many of my friends: simple waves and teased bangs as high as we could make them. It worked for me and didn't make me any more awkward than my 14-year-old self already was.

But then, as I usually do, I got a little cocky. Somehow, I thought I could pull off a spiral perm and know how to style it. I wanted to take it to the next level.

I blame it on Kylie Minogue and Whitney Houston. I remember watching them both on television, and they looked adorable with their big hair teased out and pushed off their face with a colorful headband.

So, as my first perm grew out, I begged my mom to let me get another, a bigger and better perm from her hair stylist, Becky. This was a big deal, because perms were expensive, and I did not have the money to pay for it myself. When I told my mom (also a perm aficionado) that I wanted the expensive spiral perm, the costliest one at the time, my mom continued to ask me if I was sure I would like it, but I could not be swayed.

After weeks of begging and promising I would never ask for anything else as long as I lived, my mother relented. She agreed to book me an appointment as a birthday gift with the caveat that if I decided I didn't like it, I had to live with it because money didn't grow on trees.

I was so excited when I sat down in that round chair and showed my sophisticated stylist some photos of the hair I wanted that I pulled from *Seventeen* magazine.

"I want to be able to wear my hair like that," I pointed to a beautiful young girl with gigantic, poofy hair pushed off her face with a cute bandana. "I want everything to spiral."

To Becky's credit, she tried to talk me out of it. (Sidenote: she also tried to talk me out of getting the Jennifer Aniston haircut in the mid-'90s, which also did not turn out well.) She explained why doing my bangs in the tight spiral might be a bad idea, and that getting my hair to look like the photos could be challenging, but I heard none of it. I had a bottle of Aussie Curl spray at home, and I was ready to use it.

Of course, you know how it turned out. Despite how much I used my hair pick and diffuser and Aqua Net to get my bangs just the right height, there never was a time I looked like Whitney, Kylie, or any of those cute celebrity photos I brought with me that day.

I did look remarkably like someone who stuck their finger in an electrical socket, or maybe like a wet mop.

It only took me two weeks before I started cutting my bangs myself, and I started trying drugstore products to relax my perm. I eventually went into a Fantastic Sam's to get rid of some of the curls. I swear my hair had waves in it until I went to college.

To my mom's credit, she never said a word, but she never offered to help me fix it either. My insistence on getting the perm was my problem to live with and solve. It was some gangster-level parenting by my mother, who I also believe thought I looked beautiful no matter what.

But while it was a painful, regrettable experience, I learned some valuable lessons that year:

- Know your capabilities before trying something drastic with your appearance.
- Hair is not forever.
- The most important lessons you will ever learn usually come from experience.

I tried a lot of other trends during those formidable teen years. I owned one coveted pair of Guess? Jeans and several pairs of white Keds. I donned my cheerleading uniform on Fridays and wore men's boxer shorts I bought from K-Mart for the weekends. I rocked a scrunchie daily and wore shoulder pads in my dresses a few times. I found out that Doc Martens hurt my feet as much as jelly shoes, and nothing ever felt as comfortable as a sweatshirt you "borrowed" from your crush.

Each time I tried something on, I learned something new about myself. It wasn't always pretty, but I was figuring out what worked for me and, most of the time, what didn't.

The irony is not lost on me that despite missing the fashion gene, I was blessed with three daughters. I always thought I would be the mother to sons, but God answers prayers with His own special dose of humor.

It didn't take long for all three of my girls to outpace me in the fashion department, but one in particular knows how to put an entire look together from the top of her head to the shoes on her feet. I'm always amazed at how she can take what I see as disparate clothing items and make them look like they belong together.

Like many teenage girls today, she loves to shop at thrift stores with her friends. She returns with an armful of specialty T-shirts, fancy leggings, or a name-brand wallet each time she goes. She always has a vision for the pieces she picks up. "This skirt will go great with my Jordans," or "This is for my weekend look."

One Saturday, I heard my daughters downstairs talking about going thrifting later in the day. "Hey, I'll take you!" I called down. "We can grab Dunkin' on the way." We were in a busy season, and I had not spent much time with them lately. And I certainly was not above bribery to make it happen.

When we arrived at the first store, I watched my daughter wander to the men's section. She methodically looked through the shirts that hung on the metal rack. I couldn't believe my eyes when she pulled out a gigantic tan fleece pullover that I swear was also in my husband's closet off to the side.

I don't know why, but it annoyed me that she was so focused on one small rack of oversized male clothing in a store filled to the brim with cute clothes for girls her age. It was the start of fall, so I brought her over a cute cropped sweater that I thought would look great on her and an adorable flannel shirt that reminded me of something she wore often.

But she just meh-ed me and kept browsing through the racks of men's clothing.

As I flipped through a pants rack, I saw her walk by with her arms full of drab-looking garments. "Are you trying that stuff on?" I asked, trying to hide my judgment.

"Yeah, I love this leather jacket!" she said as she walked to the dressing room. It was from the men's section of the Limited.

Don't say anything, don't say anything, don't say anything, I silently chanted to myself.

Too late.

"You have a million racks of clothes at your disposal, and you want to spend your money in the men's section? What about those cute shirts over there? Or maybe you need a dress?" The words came out of my mouth before I could stop them.

She sighed, and I saw the tears instantly well up in her eyes as she walked away from me. I knew I messed up when she flung the dressing room curtain shut.

Not surprisingly, she did not come out to show me how anything fit. She emerged from the dressing room and defiantly walked to the cash register to pay for her items from the men's section.

I felt like crap. I wanted it to be a fun outing, and I ruined it, but I could not wrap my head around why she would want those clothes. It felt like a waste of money.

I wanted to make amends and show her that I was okay with what she wanted, so I asked if she would like me to pay for the three pieces she purchased. She merely shook her head, and I knew I had blown it.

TEENAGERS HAVE YET TO LEARN WHO THEY ARE

Teenagers are always trying stuff on during these years. They are trying on friendships with a variety of people. They are trying on different activities, school interests, and hobbies. They are trying on personas, social roles, and attitudes (so many attitudes). They try on new hairstyles, music choices, causes to support, and issues to be against.

They pick up identities like a hungry customer at a restaurant buffet.

They may be vegan one day, working to save the planet, and the next they're contemplating a career as a YouTuber. Or they might dream of playing sports in college and then suddenly shift to a career in photography. They might decide they are no longer interested in attending church or suddenly want to rid the world of plastic straws.

Sometimes what they try on is harmless, such as a different haircut or a new style of clothing, and sometimes it can push your personal boundaries, such as gender identity or engaging in risky behaviors.

How we respond to these shifts in their personalities, how we react when they're trying stuff on, can make or break the relationship.

While parents often view commenting on a change they see in their adolescent as "helpful advice" (in my case, why are you buying men's clothing, dear daughter?), our teenagers process this as criticism, disappointment, and rejection. It can fracture your relationship and create a space the size of the Grand Canyon between the two of you.

It may sound like the following:

- *Are you sure you want to hang around that boy? I heard he's trouble.*
- *Why are you spending your time making videos when you should be practicing your violin?*
- *You don't want to stop eating dairy; that's ridiculous.*
- *Why don't you wear some color? All that black makes you look Goth.*
- *You don't want to quit volleyball. You've worked so hard, and you'll regret it.*
- *You aren't coloring your hair purple. What would people think?*
- *Why are you wasting your time on those stupid video games?*

It's tough not to react to these sudden shifts in their personalities with fear and withhold from what-iffing yourself.

"What if I let them quit something and they miss out?" or "What if their friends are a bad influence?" or "What if they're going down the wrong path?"

This fear can become all-consuming and cause you to forget who your child is at their core.

Our teens need us less during this time to make suggestions or point them toward where we want them to go. When they're trying stuff on, pushing back, or making decisions on their own, it's how they grow through it that matters. It's how they learn who they want to be in this world.

It's tough not to take it personally, and it's tough to lose control. It's tough to sit back and let them make mistakes.

And sometimes we have to do an internal check about what's really bugging us as parents, like how did it make me feel that my daughter was wearing drab men's clothing around town.

Sometimes we want our kids to project a certain image to the world on our behalf, and when they don't, we can feel embarrassed. It might be hard to explain to your business associates why your daughter has blue hair, or you might find it challenging to share with your neighbors that your son isn't attending college because he wants to pursue a career as a tattoo artist.

We won't always like what they are trying on, but how will they know what they like if we don't allow them to see how it fits? How will they discover who they are meant to be? How will they discover what brings them peace, joy, and fulfillment? How will they learn to stand on their own two feet?

And most importantly, how will they know we love them unconditionally if we are constantly telling them they're wrong about their choices, opinions, and beliefs?

This is tough for so many parents, especially those of us who grew up in conservative, authoritarian households. I remember my dad blowing a gasket when I double-pierced my ears at the end of tenth grade.

It was a silly battle to have, but my father was old-school and believed double-pierced ears were some sort of symbolism for how I presented myself to the world. But what I think it was really about was losing control over my decisions.

Fast forward 25ish years, and I faced a similar situation when two of my middle school daughters begged me to use their money to dye their hair, one purple and the other turquoise. I shocked myself when at first I hesitated.

They explained why they wanted something more permanent and bright than the hair chalk and temporary color I bought them the previous summer. They researched how to take care of it and even dyes that would not damage their hair. They understood that it was something they couldn't take back once it was done.

I didn't say yes immediately. I loved how their long hair looked, and I thought they might regret changing their appearance so drastically (chalk it up to my perm trauma). Because I am somewhat conservative in my own appearance, I briefly thought about how their hair might reflect on me.

But then I remembered how my dad reacted when he saw my ears (and how desperately I wanted that perm back in the day), and I knew I wanted to do things differently. So I took them to the salon, and they went all-in with the hair color—and, of course, they loved it.

What was so interesting that day, though, was a conversation I had with an older woman who was in the waiting area when we were paying our bill. She approached me with curlers in her hair and leaned in close to say, "You are a smart mom for doing this. Young people have so little say over their lives. When we give them a bit, we lend some balance to the relationship. This will pay off for you in the long run."

On the drive home from the salon, my daughters profusely thanked me. While it warmed my heart to see them so happy checking themselves out in the mirror and snapping selfies on my phone, I also told them, "Remember that you thought I was going to say no, but we discussed it and then came to a solution together. Before you go off and make big decisions, remember we can always talk about it first—even if you think I'll say no. Give me the same chance I gave you to explain yourself."

Letting them try stuff on does not mean we let them flit from thing to thing without taking ownership and accountability for their commitments. We can set rules and boundaries around their choices, but we must refrain from questioning or shooting down their opinions as they figure out who they want to be in this world. We need to be a place where they feel confident that we love and support them—no matter what they try on that day.

YOU MAY BE SURPRISED WHERE THEY START OFF AND END UP

Keep in mind that many of these new interests may be temporary. Tweens and teens can change friend groups simply by moving to a different lunch table. They might have once loved country music but are now obsessed with hip-hop. They might want to fight for a cause, join a political party, or change religions. They might become obsessed with a movie star or want to rally against the establishment. Their sunshiny disposition may change to more reflective and serious.

My youngest was a vegetarian for about nine months (although we say she was a carbotarian because she seemed more drawn to carbohydrates than vegetables). It was upsetting to me because I felt like she was not eating in a healthy way, but I kept trying to find foods she would try. She joined a gym and was regularly working out and playing soccer, so nutrition was important.

One day as I watched her eat another bowl of buttered noodles with parmesan cheese, I told her she needed to consider her diet again. "Don't worry, Mom. I think I'm going to start eating meat again. We were talking about how important protein was at the gym today."

Sometimes our best advice will never be heard by our kids because it comes from us. They need to try stuff on, compare notes with others, and figure it out for themselves. And in doing all this trying on, they are growing up and growing out of our shadows, just like I had to grow out that spiral perm.

While this paradigm shift in your relationship can be challenging and terrifying, it can also be a beautiful way to bond with your big kids and let them know you love them exactly for who they are, no matter what.

And there is no greater gift you can give your child than that.

SOMETIMES WHAT THEY TRY ON IS A PERFECT FIT

A few days after our thrifting trip, my daughter was going out to the movies with a few of her friends. She bounded down the stairs with her long hair slicked back in a high pony, deep red leggings, a cute white T-shirt, and the leather jacket she purchased with $15 of her own money.

She looked perfect. In my wildest dreams, I could not imagine how she would pull all of that together, but she knew. I should have believed in her.

My daughter holds her life like a kaleidoscope, constantly shaking and shifting to create a different picture each day. You never know what you are going to get. She is trying to find what makes her feel good, what makes her glow, what makes her love her life.

My job is to share in that discovery as she moves the pieces around to form the person she wants to be, to stick with her as she continues to find herself.

It's not always easy. I don't always like her choices, and I don't always trust her judgments. Still, I try to remember it's how she grows through it, how she recovers from her mistakes, how she learns from the consequences that will help her most in this life. If I keep my confidence in her, she will believe in herself.

And in those rare moments she asks for or needs my help, I recognize I still have an opportunity to share my values, my insights, and my beliefs. I can still model what I think is important. I still have the chance to help her become the best version of herself while developing a strong sense of self.

It can be hard when your child, who used to seek your approval on everything, starts pushing back at every juncture. However, something I had to come to terms with is that an easier relationship with me doesn't necessarily translate to a more productive and stable adult. Letting my daughter make her own choices and learning from her mistakes will be the glue that keeps our relationship intact.

Like a kaleidoscope, the pieces always settle just as they should and turn into something beautiful. Even after you get a spiral perm.

MOVING FORWARD

How can you let your teens try stuff on?

- Encourage curiosity and trying new things. Keep an open mind and allow them to pursue new interests and activities.
- Let them learn from their mistakes and experience natural consequences. If they suddenly want to participate in a theater production, they need to honor their commitment to the end, even if they find they hate it. Or, perhaps they spent their money on a guitar to take lessons with a friend, but the friend bailed. Consider encouraging your child to follow their initial interest irrespective of anyone else.
- Remember who your child is at their core. Focus on one thing each day they are doing right as opposed to what you think is wrong.
- Ask open-ended questions instead of stating judgments. For example, "Why do you want to dye your hair blue?" or "What are your favorite qualities about your new girlfriend?"

- Stay measured and pick your battles. Ask yourself if a piece of clothing or hair color is worth ruining your teen's (and your) day or if your concern for something is warranted.
- Stop worrying about what other parents will think about your parenting. As I mentioned before, our self-worth as parents should not be tied to our adolescent's choices.
- Don't become obsessed with your teen's college admissions or future. If your tweens or teens find a passion—no matter how odd or out there it seems to you—it will organically strengthen their application, or perhaps set them up for an even more successful and rewarding path. The best thing for any adolescent is to find something that lights them up on the inside and makes them get out of bed in the morning ready to do what they love. They need time and space to find it.
- Remember, it's not about you. Even if you have regrets, recall that you had your opportunity and have (hopefully) learned from your mistakes. We can't rob our teens of the chance to discover who they are simply because we know better.

  Assess and reassess your own sense of self. If you're concerned that your teen is going off on a nontraditional route, ask yourself if this is about their best interests or whether it's due to your own fear. Is it about building their self-esteem or managing your own? Are you struggling with letting your child make their own choices because you're not ready to let go? If your goal is to raise a confident adult excited to take on life, then you need to incorporate things into your life that make you feel confident and excited. We can't be dependent upon our kids to make us feel happy, satisfied, or successful, just as they can't be dependent upon us.
- Some kids simply need to find things out on their own and may rebel if they feel like they don't have a choice. Be wary of using threats to control their actions or cutting off your affection. Try to keep the communication lines open at all times.

CHAPTER EIGHT

IT'S NOT ALWAYS ABOUT THE PHONE: MANAGING TECH IN AN ALWAYS-ON WORLD

When it comes to technology, think about taking a mentoring instead of monitoring approach.
–Devorah Heitner, PhD, best-selling author of *Growing Up in Public: Coming of Age in a Digital World*

I was 24 years old when I acquired my first cell phone. As my kids like to say, that was back in the 1900s. It was a thick Nokia with a fancy leather protective case. When I purchased it, I wanted it only for emergencies. At the time, my husband and I were dating long distance, and I was driving from Washington, DC to New Jersey late at night on the weekends.

When I hit significant traffic on the New Jersey Turnpike, which was often, I would contact him so he knew I was running late. Because of roaming charges, I remember those calls costing at least four dollars, so I used that phone sparingly because my once-a-month government paycheck did not afford that kind of luxury. Most of the time, I sifted through the crevices of my car seats to find change for tolls.

Not to sound my age but, boy, have times changed. Recent survey data suggests that 42 percent of US kids have a phone by age 10, and the number climbs to 91 percent by age 14 (Rideout et al., "The Common Sense Census: Media Use by Tweens and Teens," 2021, www.commonsensemedia.org/sites/default/files/research/report/8-18-census-integrated-report-final-web_0.pdf).

Without a doubt, managing screen time is a constant burden for any parent in today's modern world. For parents of teens and tweens, phones (and other ancillary technology) are often the bane of our existence.

We worry about our kids sending inappropriate photos or connecting with a stranger online. We are concerned with unfettered access to the Internet and social media. We need to stay on top of their screentime and texting and whatever treacherous app comes out each week. We hope our kids don't participate in dangerous online challenges or get sucked into a scam. We anguish over their self-esteem as they compare their lives to their peers online, and we fear what may come across their screens next.

These issues are on top of the multitude of other problems we face when raising our big kids. For so many parents, it feels time-consuming, contentious, and overwhelming. It's so damn hard.

From my experience, the majority of parents fall into three camps when it comes to tech:

1. They hold out in allowing their child to get a device or a social media account with the hope that when they do, they can handle it.
2. They give their kid a phone for a solid reason (to communicate when at a friend's house, safety concerns, etc.) and spend an incessant amount of time monitoring messages, setting up timers and filters for screentime, negotiating on social media use, and the like.
3. They hand over a phone with the best intentions and hope for the best.

I was all three of these at one point. Once married to the principle that in no way would I give one of my children a cell phone before middle school, when my twins were in fourth grade, I suffered from a debilitating infection that left me blind in my left eye and unable to drive or even function for roughly four months.

During that period, an army of friends shuttled my kids around, but it was unnerving to rely so heavily on others. I worried that I would confuse a carpool or one of my kids would be stranded and I would not be able to get to them.

So I purchased the most basic phone for my kids to take when other people were driving them to activities. It worked out reasonably well and gave me some peace of mind. However, I opened Pandora's box.

Two and a half years later, in a drop-by visit to our wireless provider to help us with a problem my husband was having with his phone, we lost all control. The friendly salesman convinced us that upgrading his phone would be easier and more cost-effective, and we were in luck! We could get a free phone by adding a line.

After insisting we only needed one new phone, somehow we walked out with six brand-new iPhones, including one for my 75-year-old mother.

It felt like we were on an episode of Oprah. "You get a phone, and you get a phone, and *you get a phone!*"

But even though we got sucked into the marketing gimmick, we knew handing over these devices to our middle schoolers was a big deal. When we gave them out, my husband and I sat down and imposed strict guidelines, including signing a cell phone contract I found online. We told them that the phones were ours, the expectation of privacy was zero, and if you lose it, you're out a phone.

We also did not allow them to have any apps or Internet access, and I informed them that I downloaded a monitoring app onto each of their phones just in case.

"We are going to do this together to start," I remember telling them. "I don't care what your friends are doing. This is a big deal, and I need to feel comfortable in how we move forward with these phones."

Of course, they would have signed over their first-born to get their hands on those shiny iPhone 7s. At the time, it was the same as getting the keys to their first car.

It was not all smooth sailing, and my kids had some missteps even though I explained the rules over and over again in what I felt was appropriate communication.

For example, in an attempt at kindness, one of my daughters was caught trying to protect a girl whom others were talking about in a group chat. She screenshotted some comments from the group and let the girl know that she was being talked about behind her back. Of course, the girl was upset and started her own group chat with the offending girls to say that she knew she was being talked about by others. Then everyone wanted to know how she found out she was being talked about and that they had a "rat" in their group text. Eventually, my daughter had to confess that she was the one who betrayed the trust of the group by sharing private comments. It was a rough lesson for her to learn about trust in digital communication.

My other daughter needed to learn what was appropriate language and how somebody could screenshot everything she wrote and send it to someone else. After she tried out some colorful four-letter words in texts, another parent reached out to me about it and sent some screenshots of conversations she was monitoring from her child's phone.

My third struggled with some texting etiquette and keeping tabs on where her phone was. She didn't realize that not responding to a text was a big no-no at her age, so she missed out on some social opportunities.

At the end of the day, these were minor mistakes, but despite countless conversations and education, my kids still struggled with how to use their devices in an effective and responsible way.

But there were also positives in their missteps. Although some of these events seemed like a big deal at the time, they were life skills my daughters needed to work on anyway. Learning how to handle conflict, stand up for others, develop social skills, and appropriately connect with their peers are all the basics of what we want our kids to gain in middle school. Helping them grow and master these important life skills was both painful and necessary.

And that's the problem with technology. It adds another layer of complexity at an already challenging and confusing time for kids, and often in an environment that parents don't have a lot of experience with themselves.

SOCIAL MEDIA IS A GAME CHANGER

Of course, it was only a short time after handing over these devices that they started begging for Instagram. I noticed that many of their classmates who had older siblings were the ones who had some form of social media, but it made me uncomfortable. They were not ready to handle that responsibility, so we waited. They had texting, so I didn't understand what the big rush was for them to have Instagram.

As we progressed into summer, I heard my tween and young teens discuss what they were missing from not having Instagram. I discovered that many young people used social media as an initial way to connect with others at their school, especially if they didn't have their phone number. It was how they set up "hangouts," study sessions, or even meeting up somewhere to kick the soccer ball or play some hoops. I found most of the time they were sharing funny videos or celebrity posts.

But the cons still outweighed any positives. One mom shared how her daughter was the target of cyberbullying, receiving many derogatory comments through her direct messages, and another parent talked about the inappropriate content she saw come from others into her son's account.

I felt caught between a rock and a hard place.

It became even more challenging when my daughter was often left out of plans on her team because the girls often used Instagram direct messages (DMs) to communicate such information as where they would eat after a game or getting together at a tournament. They proclaimed that it was the most reliable way to communicate, particularly when the girls were using different brands of phones (iPhones versus Androids).

I was unsure, however. As someone who makes a living from social media, I felt like I had seen the worst. I didn't want my kids to be treated poorly, exposed to inappropriate content, or approached by perverts looking to lure them into a dangerous situation. I didn't want them to get sucked into the rabbit holes of social media posts that could damage their self-worth. And to be honest, I also didn't want to take the time to check their phones all the time and constantly invade their privacy. Social media felt like a dangerous bridge to cross, and I knew there was no turning back once we went over it.

The answer dawned on me one day as I snapped a photo of my precocious dog lounging on our patio furniture. I routinely posted pictures of my pup on my personal social media feeds, and my friends and family always got a kick out of it. That was when we decided my dog needed his own Instagram, and JustJax16 was born.

Set up under my email, I allowed my kids to access the account. They were allowed to post photos only of the dog and could approve friend requests of people we knew in real life. We all shared the account, but they could use it to communicate with their friends as needed.

What I recognized during that year of sharing an Instagram with my middle schoolers was that more than anything, they wanted to feel *connected* to their peers. They wanted to see their friends' photos and follow their favorite stars and athletes. They wanted to understand the funny videos that others were discussing. They wanted to be able to contribute to the same conversations. They wanted *to belong*.

I could relate to those feelings. I remembered being a middle schooler and painfully wanting to fit in with my clothing, hair, and interests. I can recall feeling dumb because I hadn't seen a particular movie or never played a certain video game. While these are not the important things in life, when you are already feeling incredibly awkward in your own skin, it can add another layer of complexity.

It was at that moment that I recognized that tech usage was more about *mentoring, not monitoring*, a phrase Devorah Heitner, PhD, regularly uses in her teachings about raising strong digital citizens.

I love this approach because it strengthens your relationship with your adolescent child instead of making it more contentious. Executing it, however, can be challenging, even for well-meaning, involved parents (definitely talking about me here). For example, even the most involved parent may miss how their tween or teen is internalizing certain information, and no one could have anticipated how the pandemic would impact tech usage.

I think the lesson, however, is that technology doesn't have to become a wedge between you and your big kids. In fact, if you teach your kids to be aware of how technology impacts their behavior, they will figure out most of it themselves.

TAKING THE PHONE OUT OF THE EQUATION

As a kid in rural New England, I had a play-outside-until-Mom-calls-you-in-for-dinner type of childhood. I rode my bike, climbed trees, and explored the woods behind my house. My friends and I would play games like Ghost in the Graveyard and wiffle ball. We spent hours making mix tapes and cutting out photos of our celebrity crushes from magazines (I'm talking about you, Ricky Schroder and Michael J. Fox).

Even though I can't imagine life without my phone now, I often must remind myself that my three children did not grow up the way I did. So one day, when my friend complained about how much time her teens spent on their phones, she exclaimed, "It's so frustrating! Don't you remember how we never had to be told to fill our time? We just did it."

But that statement isn't totally true. It's not like I always spent my downtime cleaning my room or reading books or playing outside. I also spent hours watching television on my living room floor. I could lose an entire afternoon listening to the same song over and over, trying to learn the lyrics. And it didn't take me long to get hooked on the video game console Santa gave us one Christmas.

If there was a way to waste time, I did it.

And now our kids have that same opportunity tenfold. They have millions of videos and shows at their fingertips. Spotify and other streaming music apps provide access to practically every artist out there. We can use dozens of consoles for every imaginable video game and even virtual reality.

It's so easy to forget that it's not that kids have changed so much, but the amount of available technology certainly has.

When my kids were babies, I remember buying Leapfrog toys with flashing lights and portable DVD players to help make car trips easier.

I would let my toddlers play learning games on our computer and use the iPad so I could chat with a friend. So many of their toys were battery-operated or electronic.

Technology has changed the world forever, some of it good, and some not so much. We've all heard the nightmarish stories of kids sending nude selfies to a romantic interest, communicating with strangers online, bullying or being a victim of bullying, or falling for a scam. The list of dangerous behaviors is long and terrifying.

But we need to address the root causes of these actions and not just the mechanism in which they now occur.

WE HAVE TO FOCUS ON OUR KIDS' PERSONAL GROWTH AND NOT JUST THE PHONES

Several years ago, a friend from high school shared with me that her daughter was sending revealing photos to someone she met via a messaging app called Kik. Although this mom thought her daughter's phone was locked down, the young teen somehow bypassed the monitoring software during youth camp at her church. She ended up in a blackmail scheme with another teen in England who was trying to extort money from the young girl by telling her that he would post the photos all over the Internet if she did not pay him. Luckily the young girl confessed to her mother what was happening, but the police and the FBI were engaged and it left a lasting scar on the family. Called sextortion, it's a disturbing and growing cybercrime. (For more information, see https://www.ice.gov/features/sextortion.)

While this story broke my heart, it was only later that my friend discovered how deeply seated her daughter's self-esteem issues were. When someone gave her attention and compliments, her daughter leaped at the opportunity to engage. Obviously, sending photos to strangers was awful, but at the same time, the root cause was the young girl's mental health.

Another mom friend was concerned about her son, who only met friends online and insisted they were the only people who understood him. After months of begging, she agreed to drive her 15-year-old to meet his online buddies at a coffee shop two hours away. Unfortunately, the boys had nothing in common beyond the video games they played, and the trip was a bust. The lesson learned was that her son was incredibly lonely, and she realized his social skills were less developed than those of his peers.

As parents, I believe we need to stop blaming the phone for every bad behavior and instead dig deeper into *why* our tweens and teens get sucked into certain experiences via technology. We need to remember that the device will amplify their behavior, but it isn't always the root cause.

Technology doesn't have to become a wedge between you and your big kids. In fact, if you teach them to be aware of how technology impacts their behavior, they will figure most of it out themselves.

IT'S NOT ABOUT THE TIME WE SPEND ON IT, BUT HOW WE'RE USING IT

I noticed a problem in my home a few months after we came out of the lockdown phase of the pandemic. My teens (and myself, if I'm being honest) were on our devices too much. We would be in the same room watching a show, yet we'd also be scrolling our phones. They would come home from school and then plop down somewhere to scroll on their phones. If we were in the car, they would scroll on their phones.

I noticed that everyone was snappier with each other, a little curter. There was less laughing, more biting comments, and an overall feeling of angst in our home. Their motivation to do anything vanished.

But I had three teenagers in my house, so it was to be expected, right? Between the pandemic and hormones and stress and other normal developmental issues, I figured that was the way it was because that is where we were at in this point of our lives.

Yet I couldn't shake the feeling that things were off in our home, so I started trying to address the issue. I would check in on them in their rooms and find them mindlessly watching videos or scrolling social media for hours. When I asked them to put their phones down, they usually would, but only to roam around aimlessly until I found them back up on their beds an hour later. They lost the motivation for other activities, and even when they did something else, they returned to lying down and scrolling their phones immediately upon finishing a task.

I thought I had done all the things right when it came to technology. We had specific rules to follow with consequences; I set boundaries, like no phones at bedtime or the dinner table. I felt confident they understood stranger danger and how to be kind online. But they wanted to keep scrolling or watching or listening every chance they could get.

I noticed that when my kids were stressed or sad, they used their devices as coping mechanisms, which often led to more stress and anxiety. They used them to fill time when bored, resulting in less energy or in procrastination. They used them to avoid thinking about the world around them, which numbed them. They used them out of habit.

And then, one day, my ordinarily kind and considerate daughter yelled at me out of nowhere. Another one was crying without reason. And my third didn't move off her bed all day.

Something was wrong. I was losing this battle, and close to losing the war.

My teens were struggling, and they weren't equipped to handle it. That was the day I knew we needed a change in our house. And it started with me.

You see, we can't merely tell our kids to put down their phones and expect them to know what to do next. They were raised in the era of flashing lights, digital messages, and instant gratification. They have had access to phones since birth, and we started taking photos and videos of them in the hospital room.

I remember when my kids were babies, my mom, a former nursery school teacher, would always get down on the floor with them and play. I wasn't the best at imaginary play, and I always wished they would occupy themselves for a few minutes so I could do dishes or pick up a few things. I always popped on a video when I needed to get something done, and Dora the Explorer magically came to the rescue, giving me the time and space I needed to complete whatever task I was working on at the time.

But my mom showed them how dolls could have tea parties, blocks could be a tower for a princess, and a box could turn into a fort. She explained how most kids need to exercise their imagination and learn how to use it for play. They could often figure it out themselves if you got them started in the right direction.

And she was right. Eventually, my three kids learned how to play independently and with each other. They each found things they liked to do and games they could play together. Sure, they still used the iPad and watched Dora until my ears bled, but they also knew how to entertain themselves when needed.

So when I hit this rough patch with their tech use, I returned to basics.

The first day was hard. When my kids came home from school, I stopped what I was doing and told my three teens that we were going to Dunkin'. We didn't go through the drive-thru but instead got out of the car and sat in the shop for a full 20 minutes. I asked them to keep their phones down, and they mostly complied, but I felt good that we had that time together.

Of course, they were back on their phones in the car, but I didn't say a word.

The following weekend, I made plans for us to run a few errands and fervently expressed that we should all go *together*. I may have also said we could pick up Dunkin' again. I encouraged one of my daughters to plug in her phone and play some music off her device. Then I started the questions. "Who is this artist?" and "What else do they sing?" and "Wow, how do you get so big on TikTok?"

Every day, I talked to one of my three kids about something else they could do off their phone or how to use it more constructively. Sometimes I had to carve out time; sometimes I just pointed them in the right direction. It looked something like this:

- *I looked up a new trail to hike for this weekend. You should check it out on their website.*
- *Do you want to make those cookies you saw on Insta? But we have to go to the grocery store first, so write a list.*
- *Let's watch an episode of that show you like.*
- *Do you want to go to the bookstore with me?*
- *I found this free workout app you may like.*
- *Sure, I'll drive you and your friend to X.*
- *It's your turn to take the dog for a walk.*
- *Yes, I'll go with you to the gym to sign you up. It's only $10 a month for high school students—even better!*

I slowly started showing them how much time they spent online, on what apps, and how I thought it was impacting their moods. I started working in the common area of our home to encourage them to hang out there. (They were more aware of being on their phones when not alone.) I shared some memes and videos about the benefits of spending time outside, exercise, and meditation (and received a lot of eye rolls and snarky comments).

If they talked about wanting to pursue a new activity, I pounced on it. When my daughter said she wished she hadn't quit piano, I dug out our old keyboard and showed her an app where she could learn her favorite songs for free. My other daughter enjoyed baking, so I helped her get what she needed to make videos of her projects. When another said she required volunteer hours, we did a few opportunities together, and then I helped her submit paperwork for a regular spot.

I encouraged them to make a few simple changes. They turned off notifications on their phones for social media apps, so they didn't feel the urge to check them as much. They started using timers when they wanted to scroll or watch videos to avoid losing track of time. They unfollowed or muted negative people, so their moods weren't so heavily impacted when interacting on social media.

I told them my goal was not to get them completely off their phones but to be more aware of how they used them. I hoped they would stop using them to fill voids, whether because they were bored, procrastinating, or upset. I encouraged them to look at their apps and see which ones were constructive (helped them be more active and positive, like a fitness app or podcasts) and which ones were destructive (mindless games or social media that may have a potential impact on their self-esteem).

If you're reading this thinking I'm full of crap and that this would never work with your teenagers, I get it. Please don't think my kids welcomed this behavior change with open arms and phrases like "Mom, you're the best! Thank you so much for being all over us about our screen time."

It was not easy, and it took work. Focusing on my full-time job and trying to help them fill their phone void was exhausting. There were many times I didn't feel like going someplace or figuring out what activity they would complain about the least. It was tough to be creative with ideas without spending much money. A few times I had to suffer through something that I didn't enjoy (like watching the third season of *Outer Banks*).

I commiserated with a friend who had two high schoolers but worked outside the home. Sometimes we'd take turns driving our kids to various places or host the group in our homes. She'd send me ideas late at night, like letting me know our local gym was free to high school students in the summer. I would text her, "Starbucks is half-off on Wednesdays," or "There's a free concert this weekend downtown."

I endured severe eye rolls and gigantic sighs conveying how I was ruining their lives. I rarely got all three of them involved at the same time. And the most challenging thing was modeling what I expected of them. I recognized that my digital habits weren't always the healthiest, either.

But excruciatingly slowly, I noticed a change. One day, one of my teenagers asked if I would electronically sign a form so she could get a new library card because there was a series she wanted to read. I tried not to make a big deal of it, but the fact that she started reading books for pleasure again caused me to shed a small tear. My husband then watched the movie series with her. Score!

Later that same week, two of my daughters and their friends visited a local forest preserve to watch the sunset and take photos.

I watched my daughters start going to the gym and volunteering more, writing in journals and using YouTube for sewing tutorials, learning to make their coffee concoctions, and hiking new trails. One of my daughters took Instagram off her phone (temporarily) because she didn't like how it made her feel, and another said she was picking only one social media app to keep. All three drastically reduced their weekly screen time.

And they still spent *plenty* of time on their phones, but their attitudes seemed to soften, and our connection grew.

But although it was about the phone, it wasn't all about the phone. I wanted them to have coping mechanisms for when the world was dark. I wanted them to find hobbies that would bring them joy. I wanted them to recognize when they felt sad, anxious, or overwhelmed instead of numbing it.

Now, when they have a bad day or I can tell something is wrong, I don't see them rushing into their bedrooms to sit on their phones all night. I see them going for a walk, reading, or sometimes even journaling. If I'm very lucky, they may wander into my room late at night to share what's on their minds or text me. I don't care if they send me smoke signals as long as they know I'm there to receive them.

I hope they make these choices because they no longer feel tethered to their phones, and they've rewired their brains to seek healthier ways to manage their emotions. I hope they no longer use them to soothe their young minds or hearts.

While the phone is the easiest and most accessible tool for teens to use to shut out the world, there is a litany of other ways we try to avoid what we're feeling, such as drugs, alcohol, food, shopping, and self-harm. Teaching our kids healthy ways to deal with negative emotions is a gift that keeps on giving to themselves and the people in their lives.

As parents in today's modern world, we constantly fight outside noise to keep us close to our kids. The truth is, we can complain about phones, technology, and social media; we can lament about how things were different when we were growing up; we can utilize every piece of monitoring and screentime limitation software available; and we can withhold devices and apps and games from them as long as possible.

Or we can mentor our kids on how to live in this new world order more healthily and productively—and build our relationship in the process.

MOVING FORWARD

Remember, the goal is to teach or mentor healthy tech habits, not control their screentime. Here are five ways to mentor your teens' and tweens' tech usage without a lecture:

- **Turn off all notifications but texts and reminders.** The constant pushing of information to our phones, watches, and devices is a strain on our mental health, and some experts suggest it can alter our brain chemistry. It also impacts our attention span—the constant notifications can cause a pattern called "switch cost," which is when the interruption takes our attention away from a task.

- **Routinely check screen usage.** Many health and fitness experts suggest logging what you eat or how much you exercise to see progress toward your goals. The same holds with your screen time. Many adolescents are shocked when they see in black and white how much time they spend on social media apps or watching videos, and this revelation can spur positive change. Checking this information doesn't mean you have to belittle your kid regarding how much time they spend online; instead, use it as a springboard to have a conversation.

- **HALT before you scroll.** I'm unsure where I saw this advice first, but many life coaches, therapists, and tech experts discuss this approach when trying to cut down on scrolling. HALT is an acronym traditionally used in 12-step recovery programs for substance abuse and stands for Hungry, Angry, Lonely, Tired. These four feelings are common stressors that often lead recovering addicts to participate in an activity such as drugs or alcohol, but it also applies to scrolling. Encourage your family members to pause to assess their feelings before they pick up their phones. Instead of seeking relief from the device, address what your body and mind need or want. For example, instead of turning to your phone when bored, encourage your teen to reach out to a friend or sibling to do something. If angry, turn to exercise or fresh air before distracting yourself on a device. Or consider whether you picked up your phone because you have physical needs, such as hunger or thirst, but don't feel like going downstairs.

- **Constantly assess your feed.** I was once part of a Facebook group that was incredibly negative. I told myself that I stayed in it to keep tabs on something happening in my community, but I think it was more that I became addicted to the drama and wanted to see what someone would say next. One day, when I complained about something someone posted, my young teen daughter stated, "Why don't you just leave the group?" And I really had to think about why I was in it and if I could get my information from a better source. Initially, I turned off notifications to the group. I only went in a few times a week, but I noticed within two days that my mood was better, and I was less frustrated. I then left the group entirely and never looked back. Talk to your adolescents about what and whom they are following online. Do they feel inspired or angry? Are they following accounts that are informative or inflammatory? Sometimes we need someone to point out the obvious to make good decisions for ourselves.

- **Encourage one screen at a time.** This one is tough for me, but I'm constantly working on it. My family has a bad habit of watching a movie or show while having our phones out. It's no surprise why we do this because I am constantly multitasking. Sometimes when I'm doing a mindless chore for work or at home, I'll catch up on a TV series, or I'll commit to watching a show with one of my daughters and scroll my way through it because it was a little painful for me to watch (I'm looking at you again *Outer Banks*!). But it's so bad for our brain. We are not meant to multitask, and the signal it sends to those around us is "I'm not interested." If you commit to a screen, use only that screen. It's a great habit to model, and it's great for your brain.

CHAPTER NINE

WHY IS HIGH SCHOOL SO HARD?

As far as I'm concerned, high school sucked when I went, and probably sucks now. I tend to regard people who remember it as the best four years of their lives with caution and a degree of pity.
                              −Stephen King, best-selling author

As the co-owner of a blog and social media platform that reaches millions of parents of teens and tweens each year, I'm always fascinated to see how people respond to various posts. Some people are so full of self-righteous indignation that their words take me aback. Some are mean-spirited. Some are so compassionate and empathetic that it restores my faith in humanity. And some are so full of agony for what their child is going through that I swear a piece of my heart breaks off for them.

One of our blog's most widely read pieces is a mother's anonymous essay discussing the pain associated with watching her lonely teen son get through high school. It gets me every single time.

This incredibly vulnerable piece details how her son appears to be okay on the outside, muddling through his days filled with school and activities, but doesn't have any close friends, nor does he get invited to participate in social outings. The parents try to do all the right things; they encourage him to join activities, invite others to hang out, and put himself out there. Still, he can't seem to find a supportive group or even one close friend.

This is the line that gutted me, however: "In my son's case, it's not that people go out of their way to exclude him. It's just that most of the time, his peers don't seem to notice or remember him. In fact, I think he's rarely thought of at all."

This post went viral on social media, and the commenters fell mainly into two camps. The first is the tens of thousands of parents who say, "This is my teen." So many parents share the same story.

The second is "You need to do X for your teen, such as join a club, homeschool, get a job, participate in a sport, volunteer," etc. Well, duh.

This group of commenters always frustrates me. I know they are well-meaning, but if you have ever walked through a struggle with your teen, if you feel like you've tried your best to guide them through something hard, if you've ever wanted to help your child so badly yet you feel helpless, sometimes someone stating the obvious feels like a slap in the face.

The first time this piece went viral on our Facebook page, I remember reading the comment of a nice woman who wrote a lengthy message about how every boy should be in Scouts and how she had never heard of anyone being lonely who was in Scouts and how great Scouts was for her son.

But you know what happened next: person after person started replying that their son had a problem in Scouts. "The biggest bully in town was in our troop." Or "Our leader played favorites and made it worse for our son."

Of course, this has nothing to do with the value of Scouts but the unique experience each person has in it. There is no constant to any activity, and the dynamic is always different. Sometimes it just boils down to the luck of the draw.

When raising adolescents, particularly in high school, there is no blueprint, and what works for one family can be a source of pain for another. Multiple kids from the same family may attend the same high school, but their experiences can differ completely.

IT HELPS TO REMEMBER THAT HIGH SCHOOL IS TOUGH FOR EVERYONE

I recall sitting with a group of moms at one of my twin daughters' senior banquets. We casually chatted about the girls' future plans and how fast time traveled. We paused when we saw a flood of photos, some even from elementary school, on the screen before us.

It was hard not to get choked up. It reminded us of how much our kids had grown, what we lost during the pandemic, and the impending end of an era.

When the slideshow was over, we all dabbed our eyes. Then one of the parents earnestly said, "I can't believe it's done, and I know I shouldn't say this, but I can't wait for high school to be over for my kid."

And that's when several parents nodded their heads in solidarity, and I said to myself, "Same." I was surprised by this mom's confession, and the truth was, I had thought I was the only one at that table to feel that way.

Her daughter seemed to thrive in high school. I knew she was a good student, had many friends, and participated in various extracurricular activities, so it shocked me when she made that bold statement.

We walked out to the parking lot together, and she shared that high school was a roller coaster for her daughter. She had the same friend group since sixth grade and couldn't break away from some toxic friendships. She felt trapped because of proximity and couldn't branch out to grow as a person.

From the mom's perspective, it greatly strained their relationship. She was frustrated that her daughter was stuck in a continuous loop of drama with friends who did not have her best interest at heart, and her daughter wanted nothing more than to break away.

It all felt very relatable. I thought this mom and I had nothing in common, but it reminded me yet again that no one is immune to struggling with our teens—even when it looks attractive from the outside.

ALL HIGH SCHOOL EXPERIENCES ARE NOT THE SAME

Right before the pandemic started, a study released by the Yale Center for Emotional Intelligence and the Yale Child Study Center found that nearly three-quarters of US high school students have negative feelings during their day. In a nationwide survey of 21,678 US high school students, nearly 75% of the students' self-reported feelings related to school were negative (https://www.sciencedirect.com/science/article/abs/pii/S0959475218304444). Since that study, there has been report after report that our teens are suffering during this critical developmental time.

It's not unusual for kids not to like school. I mean, who wants to get up at 5:30 a.m. and listen to someone else talk for seven hours? It's like being forced to go to a concert where you hate the music every single day.

But it's more than that for today's teens. Some of the things I've heard from parents (and experienced myself) include the following issues.

School Stress

Whether you're a snowplow parent who wants to clear the path for their kids, or you take a "let's just see what happens" approach, teens feel the tension when they're at school. There is constant chatter about getting into college, taking the most difficult classes, and building a resume. Terms like *rigor*, *challenging*, *advanced placement*, and *dual credit* are pushed into the academic landscape much more than *balance*, *practical*, or even *beneficial*.

Whether you homeschool, attend a private program, or go to a public high school, the expectations are high. As one mom I know said, "I suggested my daughter take grade-level math, and people seemed to think it was a dirty word."

It's not just hyperbole. According to an EdWeek Research Center Survey from September 2023, high school students listed stress related to finishing schoolwork/homework (34%) and grades/test results (28%) as their top two factors negatively impacting their mental health (https://www.edweek.org/leadership/why-america-has-a-youth-mental-health-crisis-and-how-schools-can-help/2023/10).

Even gym class focuses more on literary skills and sports history than movement. I saw this firsthand. I remember encouraging all three of my daughters to take yoga when it became available at our high school. I believed it would be a great way to start their day and learn mindfulness while fulfilling their gym requirement. Unfortunately, they spent much more time teaching terminology and meeting conditioning requirements than inner peace.

In addition to feeling the weight of academics, today's high schoolers often need to fill every waking hour with some activity that requires practice time, meetings, or additional work. They are expected to master everything and always perform and contribute at a high level, from volunteering for community service and joining special interest clubs to playing sports and learning a language.

We have defined success as being only the best and pushing yourself, and it is killing our kids.

The constant pressure to do more and be more is causing stress that students do not know how to mitigate. There is a reason that the best and brightest young athletes at both the collegiate and professional levels are begging us to talk about mental health.

We don't encourage balance for our high schoolers. We don't encourage self-care. We don't prioritize sleep and rest. We don't push them to pursue their passions.

And worst of all, we don't teach them to manage their stress. We just keep adding to it.

During this critical development time, it's no wonder that some teens respond by burning out, while others simply react by shutting down, which looks a lot like a lack of motivation or laziness.

The People

Let's be honest; we can't expect to force 2,000-plus kids into a school, randomly assign them classes, and then expect them to find lifelong friends who will support them. There is no place more cliquey than a high school. The socioeconomic, racial, and religious diversity in today's secondary schools also means that trying to find your people can feel like looking for a needle in a haystack. There is also not enough time in between standardized tests, learning targets, and assessments for our kids to develop meaningful relationships.

I know that for my threesome, some years were better than others. There were times when they felt alone in a lunchroom of 500, and times when they met someone in a class they connected with only to have everything uprooted the following year.

The drama can also be overwhelming for many kids. The constant bullying, peer pressure, and favoritism often exhibited during high school can wear on many students.

As I mentioned above, many teens find themselves pigeonholed into a certain group depending on their activities and interests. Some teens are naturally extroverts and easily grow their circle, while others may have a group but no true close friends. And some teens are just trying to make it through to the other side.

The Parents

Sorry, friends, but this one is true. It's easy to say that kids have changed, but the truth is, it's the parents.

Many aggressive parents are ruining the high school experience for other kids. Whether on the sports field, on social media, or at school events, many parents are obsessed with ensuring their kids get whatever they feel they deserve. We have all seen moms and dads berate receptionists and referees, go overboard at events, or incessantly complain. It ruins it for everyone.

Part of the problem is, as parents, we do not know how to handle the strain and stress of things happening in various areas of our lives and we misdirect it at others. Many of us feel out of control with events occurring in the world and our personal lives, and our inner conflicts spill into our kids' schools, the stands, the seats, and even social media. Sometimes we need to take stock of what's happening in our own world before trying to manage what's happening in our kids' world.

It makes for an incredibly challenging environment for teachers who are losing the ability to hold students accountable.

Additionally, many parents are so mentally exhausted from the demands of work, challenging relationships, and external pressures that they are struggling to provide the support that their adolescent child may need at home. Instead of helping their kids through their problems, they may leave their big kids attached to their electronics, feel too exhausted to provide and enforce appropriate boundaries, or model unhealthy habits and coping mechanisms.

Caregivers should not shoulder all the blame for this, but instead we need to take a hard look at what we value as a society and how we can support each other. If we want to help kids, we also have to help their parents.

But the problem is pervasive. Where once home was the "safe space" for many students to release their emotions, school is now the primary place they may feel any love and safety, meaning it is where they seek attention, affirmation, and support. While kids typically save their worst behavior for home, now the tables have turned.

High School Is a Fishbowl

Cameras are everywhere—on the phones of their peers, doorbells, school halls, and every street corner. High school is like living in a fishbowl where every move is documented for all to see.

Recently, my friend shared a video she saw on her young teen daughter's Instagram. There was a scuffle at the middle school, and the camera caught her daughter leaning against a locker, unsure which way to move. Because someone caught her on video at the scene, the principal called her down for questioning. (The girl froze because she had never seen a fight before.) It caused a lot of stress for the girl, who didn't know the perpetrators. She was in the wrong place at the wrong time.

While there are so many times students share photos and videos on social media accounts without consent, what's worse is that many adults do this, too. Many grown-ups won't hesitate to put up a video from their

Ring doorbells to shame or embarrass minors who did something wrong or stupid. While I'm not excusing bad behavior, what these adults need to realize is how it impacts an entire family or how it could impact the child's future.

When I was in high school, if I did something dumb (which was, honestly, quite often), I knew it would blow over in a few days. In today's always-on world, kids are constantly under a microscope with very little room for error. Every flaw, every misstep, every idiosyncrasy is magnified and on constant display to the world.

It must be exhausting.

It's Not Always Safe

It's not merely the risk of school shootings (although that is a huge part of it); it's the vaping, sexual misconduct, violence, and lack of resources that are putting a strain not only on our high schools, but everywhere our teens congregate. While I know many parents tout homeschooling as an alternative, many parents also talk about their older children being exposed to danger and unsavory behavior in places of employment, youth groups, malls, gyms, and so on. Feeling safe is a luxury that many teenagers today do not experience.

Varying Levels of Social Skills

We don't talk about this enough. Most neuroscientists agree that the human brain is not fully developed until the mid-20s, which means essential skills that can help a teen thrive in high school may only be available much later. For a late-blooming adolescent, or one who may not be as socially sophisticated, high school can be a daunting place.

STAYING CONNECTED DURING THESE HIGH SCHOOL YEARS

I know I sound like a naysayer. There are so many great things about high school, including thousands of incredibly hard-working and dedicated teachers, support staff, and administrators who mold our kids into productive people. But I can also empathize with why some teens dash through the door of graduation at the speed of a roadrunner.

These reasons are part of why we as parents struggle to connect with our kids during these high school years—even though it's often when they need us the most. Additionally, depending on our high school experience, it can be challenging to relate to what our kids are going through during this pivotal time.

The best approach to keeping your connection to your kids strong during this time is to follow their lead and ensure you don't make their problems worse because of your insecurities. But let me also say this is hard for *everyone*.

If your teens are struggling, if you believe they are lonely, if you see them isolated in their rooms, or if you know they sit by themselves at lunch, let me assure you that they are aware of it. They might be hyper-sensitive that they do not fit in or are not in the popular crowd. They might be trying to make the best of it. They might not want to burden you with their problems or feel embarrassed or ashamed.

They do not need us as parents to point it out in any way, shape, or form—but we can sit with them in their loneliness and pain. We can listen attentively. We can encourage them to pursue their passions. We can be understanding when they complain. We can remember that their perspective is small, but their problems feel big. We can ease their burdens. We can provide comfort. We can respect their feelings.

But we need to tread lightly in making "suggestions" for how they can solve their problems. We should avoid "if-only" comments, such as, "If only you would pay attention to your appearance, things would get better," or "If only you were more assertive, you could have more friends."

Remember, they know more about the people they are dealing with than we do and the repercussions that come with specific actions. For example, when my friend's son decided to quit the basketball team, she was convinced it was because he didn't want to practice anymore. She nagged him incessantly for weeks, only to find out that he had a major falling out with two of the boys on the team, and he did not feel comfortable being around them anymore.

Sometimes we have to believe that our kids know best, and we often do not have all the puzzle pieces.

HOW TO HELP YOUR TEEN HAVE A MORE POSITIVE HIGH SCHOOL EXPERIENCE

Remember, Connection Is About Quality, Not Quantity

My high school experience was a flurry of activity. I joined every club possible and spent every waking moment with friends. My siblings are much older than I am and they were out of the house by the time I was in middle school, so I filled that void with constant peer relationships.

My kids' family dynamic could not be more different, with only 16 months and one grade separating my three children. They always had someone to hang out with, even if it entailed arguing about something, so their peer relationships were different as well. They did not constantly seek out social outings because they often had them at home.

Having three high schoolers simultaneously, I learned that connection can be found anywhere, whether it's sports, clubs, a part-time job, places of worship, volunteering, classrooms, neighborhood, or even with Mom or Dad.

One of my daughters is more of an introvert. While she enjoys socializing, she also gets exhausted if she has to carry the conversation or do all the planning. Instead of doing something in a large group, she often had one friend over on a Friday night. She then maybe did something else over the weekend with another friend. She found this more manageable.

In the beginning, this blew my mind. My high school years were wild and crazy, but seeing how happy my daughter was during these encounters made me see that my experience did not need to be her experience. We both thrived, but in entirely different ways.

Also, you have to remain open to change. Sometimes a passion just isn't fun anymore, and even though, as parents, we can't understand it, there is often a more deeply rooted explanation that your teen may not have shared yet. It might frustrate you that your daughter dropped an activity to spend more time with friends, but you never know what may come out of it.

When they say they want to quit or try something new, take it seriously. It's okay to ask them to think about it for a few days, but you have to listen beyond their words and understand there's almost always more to the story. It's not worth ruining your relationship with your teen to convince them to stick with something. The adage that when one door closes, a window opens is so true in high school.

How to Help Them Manage Their Time and Mitigate Stress

I know I say it often, but I wish teens learned about coping mechanisms in high school. While our teens may freak out about something minor, it more likely has to do with the swirl of emotions occurring inside of them that they may not understand. As parents, it is our job to maintain our perspective because our kids have little of it and don't yet know how to deal with complex situations.

We can alleviate the pressure our teens may feel about academics by reminding them that there is much more to their lives than a test score or GPA. Encourage your students to take classes at the level they can handle and help them find ways to get assistance if necessary. Remind your child that everyone learns differently and how our brains are wired can significantly impact how you perform in school. Ensure they know that there is no number they can earn that is more important than how they treat people.

We can also help our teens look at their lives holistically and start approaching their schedules with balance as the primary objective. Have your teen write out their entire planned schedule, including how many hours per day or week they anticipate spending on each class and activity. Sometimes seeing it on paper can help them make more informed decisions.

One mom of an overachieving student made her daughter map out her calendar for a semester, insisting she put in eight hours for sleep and one hour for meals/downtime each day. The young student was shocked when she saw that there was no way she could manage all the academic classes, a part-time job, and the activities she signed up for. Together, they recognized that some small shifts could help alleviate some of the stress she would have felt in the middle of the semester.

On the flipside, if your teen is not involved in anything and seems apathetic, show them a calendar and ask them to identify some regular times that they will do something constructive or productive. It doesn't have to be complicated. It could be walking the dog each day at 4:30 or taking a workout class once a week. The goal is to give them purpose and accountability.

Maintain Strong Mental and Physical Health

We spend so much time when our kids are younger ensuring they brush their teeth, get enough sleep, and eat right. Then the teen years hit, and getting our kids to pay attention to their health and wellness seems impossible.

As a parent of the Class of Covid, with students who were freshmen the year the pandemic started, I found this so challenging. It was tough to keep my kids motivated to do anything, and who wanted to say no when everything they always looked forward to was canceled? We all slacked off on what we ate, our screentime, and many other ways to care for ourselves.

But puberty stops for no one, so not only were our kids under emotional strains, but they also were dealing with rapid physical changes that are difficult to understand while experiencing powerful hormonal fluctuations that can fuel emotions they don't know how to express.

Puberty is wild when you think about it. Their bodies are changing overnight, with hair growing out of private and not-so-private places, limbs extending rapidly, and pimples appearing everywhere. Their brains develop differently, so their cognitive functioning limits their ability to reason and control their impulsive behavior. Many cannot make responsible decisions in difficult situations, leading to negative consequences.

Teens are still kids even when they tower over us and need to learn how to care for their physical and mental health. I mean, many high school students think a Code Red Mountain Dew and some Flaming Hot Takis while scrolling TikTok is self-care.

But the truth is, many high schoolers struggle with physical exhaustion from not pacing their days with the rest they need. Some might stay isolated and sleep too much, trying to avoid the stress of dealing with issues or conflicts in their lives. Many are trying to manage mental health issues they do not understand. And yes, the phones.

The high school years are the best time for parents to teach kids how to develop effective self-care habits necessary to maintain their health and well-being, in conjunction with the social and emotional learning that is now integrated into many high school curriculums.

Because many teenagers think self-care exercises are hokey or for middle-aged boomers, it's all in the delivery and modeling of these activities. For example, one of my friends colors for anxiety relief. She encouraged her creative daughter to participate but couldn't get her interested—until she purchased a sweary coloring book that elevated the arts and crafts game. Instead of being treated like a child, her teen felt her emotions were being considered more adult-like, which made her want to participate more. They even found an app to create their own coloring pages.

Breathing exercises are also an excellent way for adolescents to regain control of their emotions and connect with their feelings. If you hear pushback from your teen, show them clips of the many athletes who meditate before meets and big games, or the musical performers who do breathing exercises before walking onstage. There's even a Taylor Swift guided meditation video available on YouTube.

Pay close attention to your high schooler during these critical years when their mental health is most vulnerable. Tune into their behaviors and create a culture of open communication where they feel comfortable approaching you with their problems.

Parents need to help their kids discern what is good for them and what is damaging, but avoid doing the work for them. Sometimes that means encouraging them to end unhealthy relationships, limiting academic work, restricting social media use, and finding alternative options in less competitive extracurricular activities. Other times it might mean engaging in more outside activities that are productive and good for them, trying something new that might help with their self-motivation, and making new friends. Guide them in making these hard decisions until they have the wisdom, maturity, confidence, and courage to decide what's best for them.

Ultimately, we want our kids to be healthy and well, and learn the best ways to care for themselves.

How to Manage Technology

Not to beat a dead horse, but managing technology might be the most significant mental health skill we can give our teens, but it sure ain't easy.

I'm guessing your high schooler doesn't need lessons in how to use their phone or video game console, but they do need boundaries and safety guidelines. It's like learning how to drive a car—we can't hand over the keys to someone who hasn't spent time behind the wheel with an experienced teacher.

No teen will thank you for setting boundaries today, but it could impact the rest of their lives positively.

As we've discussed, the end goal shouldn't be to monitor your high schooler every second. Instead, we must teach our kids how to use their tech constructively. As a reminder, a few simple tech boundaries that everyone can adhere to include:

- Keeping phones out of bedrooms at night.
- Turning off notifications.
- Maintaining family tech boundaries, such as no phones at mealtimes or screen-free Sundays (at least for a few hours).
- Talk about healthier coping mechanisms when feeling tired or stressed that replace scrolling, such as walking, exercising, and so on.

MOVING FORWARD

- In order to stay connected to your high school student, you first need to understand the stress and external factors they deal with each day. It's important to respond to their trials and tribulations with compassion and remember that they do not yet have the life perspective to understand that their problems are small in the grand scheme of things.

- High school can be a very challenging place for many teens today. If they come to you with a problem, do not minimize it. Instead, ask questions and take the information seriously. They may not know how to approach you or communicate their feelings appropriately.

- High school provides many opportunities to teach your teens important life skills, such as self-advocacy, conflict resolution, coping mechanisms, and emotional regulation. Stay available and practice active listening.

- Many parents are also under extreme stress during this time. Try to remain empathetic to other parents and reserve judgment.

CHAPTER TEN

WHEN YOU FEEL LIKE A BAD MOM

Parenting teens is just a season. Hurricane season!
—Whitney Fleming

A hard truth about parenting in today's modern age is that there are few opportunities to feel successful and a million ways to feel like a failure.

When my kids were young, I carried guilt around like a handbag everywhere I went. There's no shortage of things to feel guilty about when you're a mom.

I worked part-time, so my kids spent 15 to 20 hours a week with a babysitter.

My house needed to be cleaner.

I yelled too much.

My kids ate too much processed macaroni and cheese. I ate too much of their leftover mac and cheese.

They watched too much TV and didn't spend enough time outside.

I didn't spend enough quality time with each of my kids. Or my husband. Or my friends. Or on myself.

I didn't exercise enough, drank too much wine, and ate too many carbs.

I spoiled them. I did not give them enough.

One of my daughters had a few developmental delays because of a mild case of cerebral palsy, and I felt guilty wanting to do more to help her. I felt guilty about always having to bring my other two daughters with me to therapy and doctors' appointments. I felt guilty that my daughter's medical issues might be because of something I did during my pregnancy (spoiler alert: we'll never know).

That feeling of failing my kids was a dark cloud that stuck with me, storming in whenever I was stressed or anxious.

Intellectually, I knew I was a decent parent. My kids had a roof over their heads and food in their bellies. They went to school and did their homework. I loved them with every fiber of my being. But I still often worried about their upbringing and never felt that I was doing enough or doing it right. I didn't quite expect perfection, but I always believed that I could be doing more and doing it better.

As my three daughters grew, and we entered the sweet spot—that period in elementary school when your kids can play independently and think you hung the moon—I hit my groove, and the guilt slightly subsided. Those were a good few years.

Then my kids hit puberty, and I found that there was an entirely new level of guilt yet to be experienced. Every argument I had with my kids left me feeling like a failure, every barb felt like an indictment that I had no idea what I was doing, and every closed bedroom door was a reminder that I couldn't get it right.

I always worried. I worried about big things I had no control over and little things I knew didn't matter. I couldn't figure out how to get my girls to open up to me. I picked all the wrong battles.

I felt so alone. I felt exhausted. I felt not enough.

This constant feeling that I was a bad mom was toxic and ended up becoming a self-fulfilling prophecy. The more I felt like a failure and isolated myself from others, the less I could control my emotions and help my adolescent children learn to control theirs.

The truth was that while my kids' behavior hurt, it was the thoughts I believed about myself that were the real problem.

NO ONE CAN MAKE YOU FEEL AS BAD ABOUT YOUR PARENTING AS A TEENAGER

A few friends gathered at my house one Friday evening to catch up on life. We all were raising high schoolers, and our schedules were so busy that it had been a few months since we could all meet.

As we sat at my kitchen counter and shared news about jobs and health and our kids' activities, I remember one of my friends suddenly blurted out, "You're not going to believe this. My daughter stole my credit card and racked up $400 worth of clothing and cosmetic purchases, including an expensive new purse. I feel like such an idiot. I wasn't paying attention. How did I miss this?"

Before I could process the information, another friend shared that she found several liquor bottles in her basement after her ninth-grade son had a sleepover.

I could empathize with my friends. It had been a rough few weeks with my teenagers as well, including finding out about a secret social media account one of my daughters had on TikTok and some struggles my other daughter was having in her friend group.

We all felt stupid. We all felt ashamed. We all felt like bad moms. We tried to boost each other up, but it was hard. No one knew exactly what to do next.

At that moment, managing our first-born teenagers and coming out of a pandemic, I think we all felt terrible for our kids because they were facing difficult odds. Our state had recently lifted lockdown protocols, and we wanted to give our kids the social opportunities they were not afforded for nearly two years. Several were struggling with mental health challenges of varying degrees. We all were starting to think about how fast high school graduation was racing toward us.

It felt like a no-win situation. We wanted them to learn life lessons, but we could also understand why they made so many mistakes. We were disappointed in their behavior but had compassion for it. We wanted to address their missteps without pushing them down even more.

No one knew what the right next move was.

So, as we watched our teenagers act out, we all felt some guilt. We all felt like we were failing as parents. We all felt like we were bad moms.

And sometimes those feelings of failure paralyze us, rendering us unable to act because of the fear of judgment that awaits us from other parents, and, worse, the judgment we make about our own parenting skills.

In today's overly critical, achievement-based culture, it's hard to remember that the vast majority of parents are doing the best they can. They try to be conscientious and loving and raise their kids to the best of their abilities.

Yet we still forget that sometimes teens and tweens lose their way despite their parents' best efforts. I'm not saying that parents aren't the most significant influence on their kids, but once your child starts going out into the world on their own, there is a limit to what we can control.

We have to remember that addiction can be genetic. Violence could be linked to a traumatic event not related to the parents. Stealing could be attention-seeking behavior. Lying is testing boundaries. A bad attitude can be symptomatic of stress or anxiety. Promiscuity could be related to self-esteem. Pushing limits is normal. Vandalism could be a lack of impulse control.

These are not excuses, but there is always more to a story than the information we hear from the gossip train. I am confident that I didn't know how to parent during a pandemic or even after it subsided.

But also, teens in all situations and walks of life are often bad decision-makers (thanks to that pesky, slow-developing brain and hormones), especially if they feel pressured, stressed, or seek approval from their peers.

So when our teens make those mistakes, it's not always the parent's fault. Or even if we could have done something differently, that doesn't mean your child wouldn't have made the same bad decision anyway.

Sometimes it's just the wrong choice made at the moment.

IT'S ALL PERSONAL

My mom once told me she overheard me speaking to my brother when he was home from college. I was 13 and full of myself. I explained the various ways my mom embarrassed me, from things she said to the type of car we drove. I wanted a cooler mom and wished she would leave me alone.

Needless to say, there was nothing wrong with my mom. She is adorable, kind, and has the biggest heart, but at 13 I believed I knew everything about the world and my parents knew nothing.

My mom shared that she cried for days after hearing my words. She had made a tremendous effort to provide me with a life she didn't have. Although my mother had already gone through the teen years with my brother and sister, she didn't know how I truly felt. It was a shock to her.

Of course, when my mom told me her feelings, shame lit up my cheeks. I apologized profusely and tried to make amends for my crappy behavior, blaming it on hormones and immaturity.

But even though decades have passed by and I don't remember saying those things, I do remember feeling that way. I remember wishing my family was a little cooler, wanting to be more grown-up, waiting for my life to start without my parents hovering over me.

Luckily, it was just a short phase, and it didn't take long for me to realize that I was acting like a brat and my mom was a living, breathing saint. God and karma had the last laugh, however, and blessed me with three daughters of my own. #Payback.

I think about that story a lot when I am in the weeds of parenting teens, which, to be honest, feels like every day. I think about how I broke my mother's heart and how she felt like it was her fault I felt that way.

But instead of succumbing to my attitude and shouldering the blame for my crappy behavior, my mom course-corrected all the time. She told me that when I was exceedingly belligerent, it almost always meant something was going on with my friends. She let me get away with a little more then.

If I started doing more around the house, she knew I was guilty of something and tightened the reigns. When I would shutter myself in my room, she knew I felt overwhelmed by something, so she'd give me space. And every one of those times when I hurt her a little bit, she carried it with her. She carried it for me.

That's why when experts say not to take your teen's behavior personally, I don't know how.

I understand it in theory. Teens will lash out or make bad choices, but that doesn't necessarily reflect my parenting. Sometimes they just want control or to get a rise. It could be hormones or "hanger" or simply them pushing away to grasp whatever independence they can latch onto with their outstretched arms.

But my relationship with my children is the most personal thing in the world to me, and to say their words and actions don't hurt would be a lie. Sometimes a mere look can shatter my heart like a glass dropped on a tile floor.

It's easy to blame ourselves. I often tell myself that I'm too emotional, too invested, too sensitive. Still, honestly, I don't know how to parent any other way. I'm not even sure if I would want to do so.

Instead of saying not to take it personally, I wish we could lean on each other. Instead of feeling like we're at fault, I wish we could acknowledge that there will be times when your teen strikes you where it hurts, perhaps even where you are the most vulnerable. Instead of feeling like bad parents, I wish we could recognize that no one knows what they're doing.

We can admit that parenting adolescents is hard, and we're trying to learn how to love through it. We can share how we learn not to respond to their outbursts but instead teach them how to manage their emotions. We can acknowledge our shortcomings but remind each other that we're doing our best with what we have.

Let's admit that watching your teen make bad choices is gut-wrenching but a necessary part of the growing-up process, and that some will make bigger mistakes than others. Let's start supporting each other through those times when our teens break our hearts so we can focus on moving forward. Let's stop judging how another parent does it and believe there is always so much more to the story than we will ever know.

No one comes out unscathed during these teenage years. Every one of us is going through it, feeling it, trying to figure out what we're doing wrong.

It's all personal.

I'm not proud that I hurt my sweet mom, but I'm glad she never gave up on me. I'm so happy she didn't respond in kind and instead parented the kid in front of her at any given moment. I'm glad she called me out when I acted like an idiot, sometimes lost her temper because I pushed boundaries, and coddled me when I needed it most.

She simultaneously felt every emotion as I went through it and loved me through it all. It was personal for her and part of our story.

Instead of saying don't take it personally, I wish parenting experts would say, "Your teen may break your heart, but I promise you'll survive. In fact, if you learn to hold them accountable and walk with them through it, one day, if you're lucky, your relationship will be even stronger because you felt it all—the good and the bad."

IT'S WHAT YOU DO NEXT THAT MATTERS

There is a difference between feeling hurt by your teen's behavior and taking the blame for your teen's behavior. When you blame yourself for your teen's behavior and choices, you make it harder to take an essential next step: *learning from and changing the behavior so it doesn't happen again.*

For many of us, myself included, guilt and feeling responsible for your teen's behavior can become a bad habit and almost a reflexive response. Every misstep your teen makes becomes your misstep as well.

How do you know you're doing this? It may look something like this:

- *I forgot to remind my son to clean his room. I have to do a better job of reminding him.*
- *If I had punished her more for lying when she was younger, she wouldn't do it now.*
- *My daughter wouldn't be so disrespectful if I didn't work so much and was around more.*
- *My son wouldn't have been drinking at a party if I monitored him more closely.*

- *It's my fault my teen failed a class. I should have helped them more with their schoolwork.*
- *I let my teen get away with too much because my parents were so strict.*
- *I'm going to take my daughter's sports bag to her because I didn't bring it out of the car.*
- *My son yelled at me because I nagged him to pick up his shoes.*

We all want to rationalize our kids' behavior, but when does change and growth happen if we always take the blame?

I get it. It's natural to feel some negative emotions when your teen acts out, and I think it's important to reflect on your role in the situation. But guilt and constant self-blame also cloud your judgment and ability to determine what to do next. It also focuses your time and energy on what you did wrong, as opposed to holding your teen accountable for their choices so it doesn't happen again.

(Parenting pro tip: It's also critical to remember that a savvy teen can smell your guilt from a mile away and will use it to their advantage. Don't let them!)

Instead, we need to take the opportunity to walk through these challenging issues with our adolescent children. Whether they are giant mistakes or minor missteps, we must change the conversation from "I can't believe what my teen did" to "How can we learn from this and come out the other side?" As I've heard a few times, a teen has to mess up to grow up.

Where do you start?

When we're in a struggling relationship with our teens, it's like walking on ice. You can be strolling along just fine, and then bam! You fall on your tush before you even know what happened. While you may not be able to change their behavior immediately, you can change yours, which may make you feel like you've regained your footing.

Here are some tips that helped me when I felt like I was in a bad spiral and everything I did was wrong with my adolescent children:

- **Change your reaction time.**

  My husband and I have a running joke that self-awareness is a superpower. Many of us instinctively blame our problems on others instead of seeing our role in a situation. In today's world, where we're all running at warp speed to get things done and information comes at us from all directions, we constantly react and never assess.

  This was a massive part of my problem as a parent during my kids' early teen years. I would overreact first and ask questions later. This was not the way to have a productive relationship with my kids or encourage open communication.

  It may sound distorted, but what reframed my mindset and helped me was expecting my teens to mess up—because that's what they're supposed to do during these years. It was a "hope for the best but expect them to make a mistake" approach.

  Changing my mindset helped me feel more prepared to take a step back when there was a problem. When you know your teen made a bad decision, do your best to take a breath and try to understand what happened from your child's perspective. Keeping a series of questions and conversation starters in your back pocket when/if your teen gets in trouble can be a big help, such as "Did anyone get hurt?" "Who else was involved?" "Tell me your side of the story?" and even "Start from the beginning and tell me everything."

  Providing your children with the opportunity to explain themselves (no matter how angry you are or how ridiculous the situation seems at first) is a powerful way to model conflict resolution. Remember, how you deal with your kids now is most likely how they will deal with problems in their relationships in the future.

- **Big mistakes need big love.**

  One of my former colleagues once told me a story about how her son was taken to jail the summer before he went to college for using a fake ID. He was staying at his dad's home several towns away, and the sheriff decided to use him to make a statement to the other local teens that they were cracking down on underage drinking, so he had to spend the night in the county facility.

The mom drove an hour in the middle of the night to be there for his release in the early morning. Without lectures or admonishment, she drove him home and let him sleep for a few hours before they talked about what happened.

I admired her so much for the way she handled it. The young man suffered some severe consequences, including losing a spot in a music program and working off his fine and legal fees, but she led with love while he learned from it. She did not make the incident an indictment of her parenting, and she did not withhold her love and affection because of his mistake.

No matter what our teens do, showing our unconditional love is essential. It doesn't mean we ignore their mistakes or don't issue consequences, but it's also important to remember that our teens are often terrified when they make a mistake and probably do not enjoy disappointing us either.

- **Don't isolate yourself.**

  Often, when a parent has an adolescent going through a tough time, they withdraw from others. I get it. No one wants to feel judged, and sharing details can embarrass everyone in the family. And sometimes it is not our story to tell, so maintaining privacy is integral to keeping a solid relationship with our kids.

  But when we are constantly alone with our thoughts, they often become magnified, and we cannot escape our feelings of failure. We can catastrophize small problems and turn them into something larger. We can speculate about what others are thinking. We can only focus on the negative.

I know it can be challenging to share our big kids' missteps. Sometimes there are privacy concerns, or they could lead to even greater problems at school or in their future endeavors.

If you don't have a friend you can trust, finding a trusted confidant, therapist, or counselor can truly help during these times. Sometimes we just need to talk something out and gain a fresh perspective to move from guilt to holding our teens accountable.

And when we can be vulnerable with others, we should take that opportunity. Vulnerability and honesty about the challenges in your relationships aren't humiliating; they're humbling. Talking about our struggles isn't a sign of weakness but a way to heal. Sharing our personal stories isn't gossip; it's helping someone else see their world differently.

Also, when we model this for our teens, we show that vulnerability isn't a sign of weakness but a show of strength, self-actualization, and an opportunity for personal growth. Every step we take to healing ourselves is modeling constructive behavior for our teens.

- **Lean in to learn more.**

    While you may want to do some self-assessment to figure out if you had a supporting role in your teenager's mistake (e.g., maybe you did not have clear boundaries or perhaps you did give a little too much freedom too early), mistakes are also an excellent opportunity to figure out if there's more to your child's behavior than simply making a bad choice.

    For example, perhaps your child is experimenting with alcohol because they're trying to numb their feelings about a bad breakup. Or maybe they cheated on a test because they feel stressed about getting into college. Or they may have lied about where they were because they did not want to receive a lecture. The point is that every misstep is also an opportunity to learn about what's going on in your child's world and how you can help them handle their problems more effectively.

- **Let them take responsibility.**

Nothing is harder than watching our teens struggle, and some struggle more than others. Some teenagers will absolutely not learn until they fall on their faces (and then they'll probably still blame it on you!). With some teens you can tell them the stove is hot, but they won't believe it until they touch it. *I speak from experience.*

Mistakes are a good thing because they teach us how to recover. The fastest way to reduce your guilt about your child's behavior is to make sure they learn how to be accountable for it.

Something I learned from talking to a writer friend and therapist is that discipline with teenagers is complicated. While most of us understand that we need to give our kids more freedom and responsibility, the problem lies with knowing what to do when they abuse their privileges and ignore boundaries.

A problem with raising adolescents is that you can no longer "force" your kids to do certain things. I remember when my friend's six-foot son once refused to go to a family event. I laughed when she said, "What was I supposed to do? Pick him up and carry him down the stairs? I had to be there, so I went and he got his way." There are times when we can't make our defiant teens do what we want them to, no matter how hard we try.

In my case, at the onset of these tween and teen years, my first instinct was always to take away their phone. This was complicated because their schoolwork was often on an app on their phone. Their music was on their phone. Their calendar was on their phone. They received messages from teachers and coaches on their phone. It also led to more sneaking around and lying.

My next tactic was to do what my parents always did, and ground them from social outings or doing something fun. This seemed to make our relationship worse and more contentious, and most times it didn't even seem to faze them. I also couldn't help thinking they would start lying to avoid getting caught, just as I had when I was their age.

The answer lies in understanding what you want your adolescent to learn from the experience and discerning the difference between punishment and consequences. It's a subtle difference that took me a while to grasp because it differs from my parents' authoritarian method.

The goal of a punishment is to make someone suffer—you didn't follow the rules, and now you need to feel bad. It's to dissuade someone from doing it the first time or doing it again. It's like going to jail for breaking the law, but we know that often doesn't work because how many repeat criminals are there?

The problem with punishments is they don't teach anything; instead, they often encourage tweens and teens to simply avoid getting caught. This was my experience as a teenager, and I became very good at it.

Conversely, consequences are more constructive, and the goal is to learn from the process. As my therapist friend told me, *punishments make parents feel good; consequences empower kids to do better* (that was a lightbulb moment for me).

But what does this look like in real life? There is a subtlety to the difference that may take some time and experience to comprehend.

Let's use a simple example. Say your teen continuously takes food into their room and leaves dirty dishes all over the house despite your warnings. A punishment would be no video games for two weeks. A consequence could be making them responsible for doing all the dishes for the family for a whole week so they can understand the effort it takes to keep a house clean. To enforce this consequence, you can tell them they cannot go anywhere or play video games until every dish is clean and put away. You may need to remove the gaming console to ensure this happens or have your child sign a contract agreeing to the terms. The end goal is for the teen to learn that it takes effort to maintain a house and clean up after everyone.

Another common problem is an older child who continuously stays out later than they are allowed. If you have a teen who routinely misses curfew, instead of grounding them from going out again, consider rolling back their curfew by an hour for a few weeks until they prove they can be responsible again, and then allow them to go back to their original curfew once they prove they can maintain it. The goal is to be reasonable and help your teenager demonstrate responsibility, not to have your child obey simply so they don't get in trouble.

- **Be real with them about your hurt feelings.**

While I believe it's important to keep a positive parent-child relationship during the teen years, adolescents must also understand that their words and actions matter. When your tween or teen lashes out or if they do something to disappoint you, it's okay to tell them how it made you feel honestly and succinctly, but make it about their actions, not who they are as a person.

There was a time I felt some awkwardness creep into my relationship with one of my daughters. It seemed no matter what I said or did, I annoyed her. One day, I finally stated, "Listen, if you have a problem with something I'm doing, I hope you will tell me. I can't address it if I don't know."

While it took a few more days, it eventually came out that there was a misunderstanding about something I said and her feelings were hurt, which caused her to harbor some resentment against me. I'm glad I didn't chalk her actions up to simple teen angst, and I confronted her behavior in a positive way. We both learned something.

I have a friend who shared how her son needed to go to rehab to kick a drug habit. She explained that a considerable part of his recovery was the two of them going to therapy together to discuss how they could move forward. She texted me, "I thought telling him that I was hurt and mad at his choices would make things worse or even push him to use drugs again, but he actually said that knowing I cared and loved him anyway made the difference for him to stay in rehab." Respect and honesty for the win!

While we don't need to acknowledge every negative emotion our kids express, modeling how to talk to someone about your feelings—and then move on in a constructive way—is a life skill they can carry with them forever. It will help them in every relationship they have.

- **Keep showing up.**

  I don't know a parent of teenagers who wouldn't say their kid sometimes pushes them away. It could be with their words, actions, or bad choices, but they are all slowly peeling back our fingers one by one to release our hold on them.

  And, of course, that is what they are supposed to do.

  But as they let go, it's our job to stay available. We do not need to be a doormat or take abuse, but we need them to know that we will be there for them in some capacity, no matter what.

  What does this look like? It means when they come into the room, put down your phone or laptop and make eye contact whenever they talk to you. It means insisting that you eat some meals together. It means checking in before bedtime and showing interest in what interests them. It means never turning your back on them, even when they show their worst.

  They are swimming to the pool's deep end but they need to know we're in the shallow area if needed. No matter what.

- **Remember, it's a season.**

  One time, my friend and I talked about how crabby our teens were and how it felt like something was in the air. She said, "This is just a tough season."

And my response was, "Yeah, hurricane season!"

But it's true. The kid who pushed you to your limit during their teen years could very well turn into your best friend and closest confidant a few years later. We just have to help them grow through it as we go through it.

How do I know this? Well, I was a teenager once too, and my mom and I are incredibly close even though I did my best to push her away.

Teenagers often come back to their parents after painfully breaking free.

MOVING FORWARD

- When you're going through a difficult period with your adolescent child, it can be easy to blame yourself. Remember that your tween or teen is learning and will make mistakes. While it is important to be self-aware, you should not shoulder the blame for every misstep your child makes.
- Focus on what you can do next more than on where you might have gone wrong. Guilt can make you focus on what you think you did wrong as opposed to helping your big kid learn from their mistakes.
- Understand the difference between punishment and consequences. (Punishments are an attempt at deterring behavior; consequences are learning why the behavior isn't appropriate.)
- It is okay to feel hurt by your tween's or teen's behavior, but don't make it about who they are as a person. It may feel personal to you, but it was more likely a bad decision by them.
- Stay available at all times, but especially when they act like they don't need you. They may desperately want independence, but it's important they know you are their flashlight to help illuminate their way when needed.

CHAPTER ELEVEN

MANAGING THE EMOTIONAL ROLLER COASTER OF RAISING TEENAGERS

You must know yourself to grow yourself.
–John C. Maxwell, best-selling author,
leadership coach, and speaker.

Disclaimer: *Managing mental health is something we should all take seriously. It is important to state here that I am only discussing how I try to maintain positive mental health habits in my own life and model these for my family. Although I try to learn about new tips and tricks to keep a strong mindset, I am not a professional, and I recommend that you seek help for a mental health–related issue or illness from a healthcare practitioner or a licensed mental health therapist when needed. I am a big believer in therapy, life coaching, and engaging others who are more knowledgeable. Getting help helps.*

There is a classic line from the television show *The Office* that comes to my mind so many times during these teenage years. In the scene, Michael Scott (played by Steve Carrell) wants to invite a Boy Scout Troop to an office party where there will be alcohol, gambling, and other adult forms of entertainment. His work colleague, Toby Flenderson, is trying to explain why he doesn't think it's a good idea. Exasperated by his negative response, Scott blurts out, "Why are you the way that you are?"

While Toby had a good reason to quash Michael's idea (I mean, Hooters was catering the event), the sentiment behind Scott's statement hits me like a sock in the gut regarding parenting teenagers.

- When I found a spoon with peanut butter on it in between my couch cushions: *Why are you the way that you are?*
- When my daughter burst into tears because I asked if she was wearing her flannel pajama bottoms to go shopping: *Why are you the way that you are?*
- When I found an ice cream bowl in my daughter's dresser drawer: *Why are you the way that you are?*
- When one of my kids lied to me about where they were even though it was not a bad place: *Why are you the way that you are?*

- When I asked them to put their phone down and they ignored me: *Why are you the way that you are?*
- When they didn't tell me they were struggling with their mental health: *Why are you the way that you are?*
- When they rolled their eyes because I asked if they were hungry: *Why are you the way that you are?*

Sometimes I was so exasperated I wanted to blurt out myself, "Why are you making it so much harder?! What is wrong with you? Why are you the way that you are?"

Why did they make it so challenging and so unfun? I know it's not the same, but it is exactly how Michael Scott felt about Toby.

I hated how I responded at times. I would get so angry that I'd yell and freak out. It would put me in a bad mood. It would ruin my day, which would ruin their day, too.

I know adolescents have frustrated their parents since the dawn of time, but I finally recognized I needed to ask myself a few follow-up questions too: "Why are you the way that you are?" brought me to "Why does it bother me so much?" and "Why do I respond that way?"

Okay, maybe I had to ask, "Why am I the way that I am?"

Lightbulb moment. Maybe it wasn't just them.

Once I started seeing my role in the issue, I recognized that having a better relationship with my three adolescent children boiled down to four things:

- Learning how to control my own emotions
- Identifying my triggers and why certain behaviors made me lose my mind
- Understanding why my children behaved in certain ways
- Developing coping strategies so we could all deal with our stress and anxieties better

CONTROLLING OUR EMOTIONS SO THEY DON'T CONTROL US

I'm not sure when I first saw this quote, or even who said it, but it sums up my life perfectly: "Sometimes the worst place you can be is your own head." I feel this quote in the depths of my soul as I have been chasing peace my entire life.

There was never a time I can remember when my mind didn't seem to be racing at an uncontrollable, frenetic pace. Overthinking is my specialty, and worrying about things outside of my control is my love language.

One day, when discussing multitasking with my daughters and why I try to do 42 things at once, my husband summarized what occurs in my head at any given moment perfectly: it's like a thousand tennis cannons shooting balls simultaneously at each other 24/7/365, and the off button broke.

There are some positives to my brain. I am a taskmaster and can get many things done in a day. It can hold a lot of useless information. I've been told I have a quick wit and am a hoot at parties.

But there are obviously some downsides, too. It has always been a struggle for me to control my emotions, and I fight to manage anxiety. I can take on other people's problems to the detriment of my mental health (shoutout to my fellow empaths out there!). Tears will often spring to my eyes before I even understand what I'm upset about, an innocuous statement can cause me to feel irritable, and I can react to a situation with too much anger and yelling.

I hate that I sometimes take out my feelings on those closest to me, and I've been working on these issues for the past two decades, which also coincides with how long I've been a parent.

Let's just say it's been a journey full of ups and downs.

I know I'm not alone. My issues are specific to me, but many parents tell me they are trying to break patterns of behavior they have carried with them throughout their lives.

That's why, without a doubt, the single best thing I ever did as a parent was to start working relentlessly on myself. I leaned into my past to understand how it impacts my behaviors and responses. I worked on understanding the triggers that cause me to lose control of my temper and rational thinking. And yes, I'm going to repeat it, I developed coping mechanisms so I could better manage my emotions so I could help my kids manage theirs.

It's not easy to keep your mental health strong in today's world, where everything seems like it's on fire. We are constantly barraged with news, images, and information about conflict and destruction. The political strife is unsettling. The climate crisis is unnerving. Violence is happening all around us, and people can't be civil toward each other.

Working on myself is the hardest, most humbling thing I've ever done. It's also been the most rewarding.

I read once that it's tough to have a good relationship with someone who does not have a good relationship with themselves, and that stuck with me. I'm obsessed with working on myself because it's the greatest gift we can give to our kids (and anyone in our lives). I believe this because I know I could have benefited greatly from learning some emotional regulation as a teen.

Growing up, I often saw adults manage stress and anxiety by smoking a pack of cigarettes a day, drinking alcohol, or getting irrationally angry at something or someone. Many of my peers followed suit, and I started to believe getting through a challenging situation always involved a little self-destruction.

In my family, as I think was the case for many, you didn't talk about problems. You just accepted what was and moved on. For some people that works. For others who are overthinkers and anxiety-ridden like me, we need some ways to deal with the tough stuff.

I think that's why some people resort to unhealthy coping mechanisms or lash out. We simply didn't know there were healthier alternatives or a different way to do things.

And in my quest for self-evaluation and discovery, after years of discussions with friends, family, and therapists, here is one thing I have learned: you can't model what you have never seen.

So, sometimes, we have to take matters into our own hands. For me, emotional regulation came easier once I recognized that so much of it is giving myself space and grace: time to pause and collect my thoughts before responding. I also needed to dig deep and believe I could do better for myself and my family.

The key is to turn your impulsive reactions into healthy responses. I read books and articles, had a million conversations, and spent a lot of time reflecting. Eventually, I came up with my own little way that helps me handle my feelings better. I call it Scratch the ITCH. It looks something like this:

You are stressed because you have a big work project due, your daughter needs black pants for a band concert, there is a basketball tournament over the weekend, you're planning for your mom's 75th birthday, and the dog needs to go to the vet. You just found out one teen left the car without gas, and the other is failing math. You walk into the house, and the kitchen is a disaster. You glance over and see your son sitting on the couch, scrolling on his phone, and you feel the vein throbbing in your head. When you ask him why he didn't clean up the mess in the kitchen, he says nonchalantly, "Bruh. I'm just trying to relax after school."

Here's what you do:

1. **Stop.** Whatever you do, don't engage. Nothing productive will come out of it. Do whatever it takes to take a pause.

2. **Identify.** As you take some time and space, try to identify what you're feeling. Displacing our emotions is a big problem in the parent-teen relationship from both sides. Are you angry at your son? Are you disappointed with your schedule? Is it just stress?

3. **Trigger management.** I talk about learning how to manage your triggers below, but once you identify them, it becomes easier to know how to deal with them. When I'm stressed, other people's messes set me off (this is common with most women). Removing myself from a room can decrease my heart rate and help me think more clearly. Sometimes your kid's behavior can trigger an emotional response. Counting to five or deep breathing for a few seconds are great resets. (A favorite scene from *Ted Lasso* is when Ted's son explains he lashed out at a friend because he didn't follow the advice: "When you're angry, count to 10. If that don't work, do it again." I always think about that quote when I need to step away.)

4. **Cope.** Sometimes, we need to do more than simply take a few deep breaths. The end goal of coping mechanisms is to stop the explosion of emotions before it starts. When I keep up with what I call *preventative coping mechanisms,* I feel more present and mindful of my feelings. I try to do these things daily to stay grounded, such as walks outside, journaling, meditation before I go to sleep, exercise, and so on. It's also a good idea to have some *escape-hatch coping mechanisms* to help us regroup during a stressful encounter, like when your kid calls you Bruh, they're late for the hundredth time, or they lash out with some backtalk when you already had a bad day. These may include things like drinking a cold glass of water, washing your hands for 45 seconds, listening to a certain song, venting to a friend, or vigorous exercise. These are healthy ways to express and respond to anger that do not take someone else down with you. If you can't remove yourself entirely from a situation, an

active distraction can reboot your brain and stop you from destructive behavior or from hurting your relationship.

5. **Home in on trouble spots.** Sometimes, we're carrying around baggage that constantly spills over into our current relationship. When you start recognizing patterns, you can begin to address complex issues that may be repeating like a bad case of heartburn.

HOW I LEARNED HOW TO UNDERSTAND MY TRIGGERS

Triggers are basically emotional responses to something in our present that relates to something in our past. While this can happen at any time (e.g., PTSD from an illness or a tragic event), a lot of parents experience triggers through their kids without ever realizing it (I'm holding up my hand in solidarity). Because parenting can be overwhelming and stressful, we often don't have the time or presence to fully comprehend what's happening, and it becomes a vicious cycle that is tough to end.

For me, the most challenging part of feeling triggered by something my big kids did was how fast I reacted in a negative way. I often yelled and started a lecture before processing what happened. Then I felt guilty for how I acted, which led to an apology and some overcompensation to the child, which taught them nothing except that their mom was a little loco.

The struggle was understanding what was happening. Controlling the speed of my brain was never my strength, so if I wanted to control my reaction time, it often boiled down to controlling my stress and anxiety. If I was feeling good and in control of my life and feeling healthy, I could handle anything. When I was stressed, and my kids added to that stress, I took it out on them. (I think it's important to underscore here that there were a lot of times my kids' behavior deserved to be addressed. I'm specifically referencing that the way I addressed it was not productive.)

Because I'm a writer, I often turn to putting pen to paper whenever I'm in a dark place. As my kids entered adolescence, they constantly exasperated me. With three daughters going through puberty at the same time, there was always someone crying, someone frustrated, someone complaining (and yes, sometimes it was me). Sometimes it felt like too much for me to carry their emotions and deal with whatever was going on in my life.

I started some basic journaling at the end of each day. Using the notes app on my phone, I would jot down how I felt during the day, including my stress, worries, and parenting regrets. I did this for roughly three weeks when I started reading things back and seeing a pattern. When things were going well for me, I was a more present and positive parent. When I was struggling, I had zero patience, and my teens broke me.

It sounds so simple, but understanding my emotional responses was key for improving my relationship with my kids and makes so much sense now. My parents were volatile like I was. We were calm, happy, and at peace in the good times. But when they were going through tough problems and challenges, they reamed me for some minor things I did.

I always think back to how understanding my dad would be if I earned a bad grade or broke curfew. My mom was the enforcer of the punishments, and it was my father who always seemed to be more compassionate. But when my dad was in a foul mood, my simply knocking over a cup could set him off on a tirade.

When I looked back at my journal, it was easy to see I started adopting a similar pattern.

I also started listening to my mind and body more. I am not anal about neatness and organization, but large amounts of clutter and mess do bother me in my home. I noticed that walking into one of my daughter's bedrooms often impacted me physically. The mess and disorganization literally would raise my heart rate. Then I'd start seeing things that would set me off, like a dirty dish or mud from some shoes. I would try to convince myself that it didn't bother me (picking and choosing battles and all that jazz), but I would carry it all day. Then, after a long day of holding these negative feelings, I would engage with her over something stupid.

Why are you the way that you are? I would think. Well, I certainly wasn't making it any better.

Finally, I had to be honest with myself. I had to admit that I was part of the problem. This was when it dawned on me that if I wanted to have a better relationship with my teens, I had to stop wondering why they were the way they were and start asking the same question of myself. I had to *scratch the itch* to make it better.

I want to retake this opportunity to underscore that if you are truly struggling with the relationship with your adolescent children, therapy or a life coach may be of great help. Sometimes your triggers can be tough to identify, but a mental health therapist who has training can help.

WHY ARE THEY THE WAY THAT THEY ARE? UNDERSTANDING YOUR TEEN'S BEHAVIOR

One time, I wrote a social media post sharing how I was trying to understand my teens' behavior so I could respond compassionately. A very salty 20-something posted a comment that said: "How can this be so hard for you? Do you not remember what it was like to be a teenager?"

And, of course, I laughed out loud. As I enter midlife, it does get more challenging for me to remember that time period. I mean, I remember the basics. I had a messy room. I wanted to spend all my time with my friends.

I couldn't wait to leave home. But why I felt a certain way during that time? It's tough to recall.

But also, raising a teenager in today's crazy and chaotic world is nothing like how I grew up. Today's teens are dealing with so many things that I never had to think about, like mass shootings, technology, intense academic pressure relating to college admissions, volatile world events, pandemics and global health issues, and climate change.

That's in addition to the normal teen stuff like peer pressure, bullying, dating, acne, drinking/drugs, and so on. They are stressed, and it's challenging to help them manage the anxiety they feel about the world around them while managing our own fears.

As adults on the outside, we don't make it easier for them either. In today's always-on social media culture, we tend to admonish and shame more than we encourage and empathize.

For example, something I notice is how quick we are to criticize today's teens. We post their poor behavior online for all to see from our cameras without any context. We call them lazy and unmotivated. We say they don't care about anything but their phones. We often talk *about* them online or in groups instead of talking *to* them. We judge their behaviors and assume the worst.

I'm reminded of the time a group of teen girls were at a Major League baseball game and roasted by sportscasters for two minutes on live television when caught taking selfies. The footage went viral and the young girls were mocked all over social media. The story came out later that they were participating in a T-Mobile promotion that was broadcast throughout the stadium.

But that type of "selfie-shaming" happens all the time. I see this sort of behavior from adults in local parenting groups and on apps such as NextDoor and Ring who post footage and photos of youth in "gotcha" moments with the intent to shame or ridicule without context or the opportunity to explain.

And then we wonder why so many adolescents are hopeless, sad, and full of despair—and why their parents struggle, too, with trying to meet unrealistic expectations from the rest of the world.

So, although I wasn't a fan of that Gen Z comment on my lack of memory of my teenage years, he was not wholly wrong either. As parents and adults, we are often caught negatively reacting to what seems like ridiculous behavior, instead of remembering that we were young and misunderstood once too.

I also think it's important to underscore the difference between understanding the "why" your teenager may be acting in a certain way and the "how" you manage it.

When I discuss the "why," many adults will get angry and think I'm offering excuses for bad behavior. And in some ways I am. But the best way to help our kids to grow through something is to understand it. Sometimes there is so much more to a behavior than meets the eye, and I think we forget that.

I saw a video once that said when you're dealing with a child of any age who is acting out, you can defuse the situation by saying, "I think we should talk about this more in a little bit, but while we both calm down, try to think about what your feelings are trying to tell you."

I thought that was brilliant. Is your anger telling you that you're mad at what a friend did or frustrated with a grade you received? Are you crying because you're sad that your mom said no to something or don't want to feel left out? Did you lash out at your younger brother because you don't like him, or because you didn't like the way someone made fun of you at school?

What are your feelings trying to tell you?

And guess what? It works for parents too. So before we decide our teens are acting disrespectful and snarky just for fun, we need to help them understand their feelings and the "why" behind them, but also why we may be responding a certain way. Was the eyeroll the straw that broke the camel's back after a long day of work? Are you frustrated that your teen son didn't put his dishes in the sink or is it that he hasn't kept up with his schoolwork? Are you mad that your daughter came home late or do you not like her friends?

What are your feelings—and reactions—trying to tell you?

Here are some things to keep in mind about why teens might be acting a certain way, especially when you say to yourself, "Why are you the way that you are?"

HORMONES AND THE TEEN BRAIN

The teen brain is a crazy thing, and because I'm not a neuroscientist (nor do I play one on TV), I'm not going to pretend to understand all the ins and outs of their cerebellum. What I can tell you is that there is scientific evidence that their erratic behavior, emotional responses, and impulse control are impacted by that big mass of gray matter and how it is developing.

I remember my husband making a joke one day to our daughter and she burst into tears. I was shocked, as we had just been laughing at a YouTube video moments before. When I asked her what was wrong, she sobbed, "I don't know!" as she ran out of the room.

It broke my heart, but I also kind of understood. As a middle-aged mom approaching menopause, sometimes my emotions get the best of me, too.

I've heard similar stories from my friends raising boys, except it usually relates to anger or apathy. We have to remember that some areas of their brain are still under construction and there is a constant surge of hormones coursing through their bodies. This can lead to mood swings, erratic behavior, and heightened emotional responses. Basically, the inside of their brain is like a Rock 'Em Sock 'Em Robot boxing match, with the different parts of their brains trying to emerge as the winner.

While this is not an excuse for disrespectful behavior, it does help to remember that their emotions explode with all these powerful feelings, making it impossible for anyone to handle them. The result is uncontrollable crying, moodiness, and attitude fluctuations. I know that Forrest Gump was talking about life in general, but raising tweens and teens is also like a box of chocolates. "You never know what you're gonna get."

Because they have poor impulse control due to the brain changes, they often express an emotion before thinking or dealing with it. (My older teen once told me that rolling her eyes was an impulse she truly struggles to control, even in school.) This can cause them to be more prone to conflicts, especially with their mothers, who are quick to forgive and their safe space to let down their guard. Some teens' emotions are bubbling at the edge like a volcano waiting to erupt, and unfortunately it's often in the home where they can no longer contain their feelings.

We must talk to our teens about what is going on with their brain and body during this time. Awareness is half the battle. We don't want to minimize their feelings, but instead teach them how to acknowledge and manage them when they feel out of control, a skill they can take with them for their entire lives.

We also have to remember that while adolescence is a specific period, teenagers mature at different rates. It's hard to imagine, but some 13-year-olds are more developmentally mature than some 18-year-olds, and some 18-year-olds are more mature than a 25-year-old. As parents, it's our job to continue to teach and model life skills, coping mechanisms, and emotional responses that will help them become productive members of society.

INFORMATION OVERLOAD

Some people don't agree with me, but I think being a teenager today is much harder than it was when I was growing up in the late '80s and early '90s, and yes, it has a lot to do with technology.

I remember eating my cereal in the morning at my kitchen counter when I was in high school. At the same time, my dad read the newspaper and watched a portion of *Good Morning America*. I would catch a few highlights of what was happening in the world and only think of it again at 6 p.m., when my parents would watch the evening news before dinner.

The average high schooler consumes infinitely more information than I did at their age, often before rolling out of bed each morning. While it's easy to dismiss that this information input is typical for teens since they mostly have grown up with it, we don't truly understand how this digital bombardment impacts their mental health.

Couple this with social media, academics, digital communication, and videos/entertainment, and there is no way teens can process all this information. Overstimulation is for real. The result is a generation of teenagers who are experiencing paralysis by analysis and overwhelming incidents of depression and anxiety.

For parents, this can be tough to manage, and there is no one-size-fits-all solution. The goal must be to help our teens understand the power of technology without succumbing to it. It involves having conversations about the risks and problems with information overload, understanding the impact it has on us physically and mentally, and my favorite, developing off-line coping mechanisms.

QUEST FOR INDEPENDENCE

Nothing is as painful as when you feel the wrath of rejection from your adolescent child. I don't care how much you know about the teen years or whether your kid is 10 or 20; it still hurts.

You may still (mostly) get along with your big kid, but you may not be as critical to their development and sense of self as you were in the past. Their friends become integral in decision-making, and it often feels like they have one foot out the door while you're trying to hang onto their pinky. And it can be exhausting to feel like you constantly exasperate them with every comment.

A friend with children older than mine once said, "Acting like they don't need you is what they're supposed to do. Knowing they still do is your job." I felt that. So, even though it sometimes feels contentious, it's not necessarily so. We don't have to fight it. We just have to stay available while they keep pushing to break out of the eggshell.

STRESS

Stress is our mental or emotional reaction to external challenges, events, or pressures. As parents, we often discount the stress our teens face. As the ones with full-time jobs, mortgages, and the responsibilities of taking care of our families, it can be challenging to remember what it was like to be in middle or high school.

But as I mentioned in earlier chapters, today's teens are not growing up in the same world, and the intensity of stress looms larger.

Teaching your tween or teen to manage their stress can be your greatest gift. If you notice your adolescent child constantly stressed to the max and it's impacting them physically or mentally, consider looking at their schedule and responsibilities to ensure they're getting enough sleep and downtime. Could you encourage them to focus on self-care? Give them permission to rest.

Also, how you model stress management will have a tremendous impact on how they manage their stress when they leave home. Be cognizant of turning to alcohol or drugs when you feel anxious or stressed in front of your older kids, and remember your actions will speak much louder than your words.

PERSONAL PROBLEMS

Teens, like anyone, face external challenges, experience stress, and have bad days. These can affect their behavior, moods, and reactions, especially with their parents.

One of the things I learned the hard way is that even if you try to do everything right with your adolescent, even if you feel like you're acting in a way where they should be comfortable coming to you with their problems, it doesn't necessarily mean they will.

Grace is an integral part of parenting tweens and teens. I've learned that giving my kids the benefit of the doubt when they lash out at me for no reason, roll their eyes, or make a snarky comment is a powerful form of love.

While I want my children to know they can always come to me, I also must accept that sometimes they don't. Most times when they act out against me, it's often because they can't control the behavior of someone else.

As someone who processes emotions by talking and writing, it's tough on my heart when my kids don't tell me what's going on in their lives. It's hard not to take it personally. It's hard for me not to constantly ask them what's wrong and if they want to talk.

But I try to remember that it's not a personal assault on me. I recognized that it takes several days, if not weeks, for one of my daughters to process events and want to discuss them. Another daughter compartmentalizes her problems until she's ready to deal with them (a trait she gets from her father). And my youngest comes to me when she needs me, and not a second before.

Learning this about my teens has been a humbling experience, but learning to step back has eventually brought us closer together. As I always tell other parents, while we should never be someone's doormat, including our teens, we can always think the best of our kids and give them a space to work out their problems on their own with the assurance that we're waiting in the wings if needed.

TUG-OF-WAR OVER RULES AND BOUNDARIES

About a decade ago, a friend I went to high school with told me she always liked staying the night at my house because she knew we had to be home by a specific time or my mom would kill us. I found that hysterical because I used to hate that I seemed to be the only person in my senior class with a curfew. "Nothing good happens after midnight," my mom always said.

"But it was awesome," my friend shared with me. "I felt like my parents let me do whatever I wanted, which was good sometimes, but when I went to your house, I felt safe and loved. I knew that's how I wanted to raise my kids."

Whoa. Sometimes all it takes is hearing something from someone else's perspective to completely flip your own.

During childhood, and especially during the teen years, parents often set boundaries to provide structure, guidance, protection, and a sense of security for their kids. These "limits" often help teens to stay safe and develop their self-worth. But let's be honest, no teenager has ever said, "Thanks, Mom, for setting all those rules for me. I love it when you tell me what I can't do!"

Teenagers think they know everything and lack perspective about the world around them. Parents often know too much and may fear everything. The tug-of-war over house rules can lead to many disagreements, name-calling, and even an occasional "I hate you!"

While many teens often believe boundaries are just rules that stop them from having fun, establishing and enforcing boundaries helps teenagers develop self-discipline, make responsible choices, and understand the consequences of their actions.

Say it with me: *Boundaries are love.*

It's tough to find the balance, and again, it's developmentally appropriate for teens to push back and think they know how to keep themselves safe. Our job is to keep extending the string so they can eventually learn how to live on their own safely and productively.

I'm not going to say it's easy, but I will say they're worth it.

THE LONG GAME OF PARENTING: TEACHING OUR BIG KIDS HOW TO COPE

I think we are failing our middle and high school students by not focusing on topics like emotional regulation, stress management, mental health awareness, self-care, and yes, coping mechanisms. We all agree that today's teens face unprecedented levels of stress and anxiety. Yet we often dismiss typical teenage worries like crushes, homework, and school activities.

We want our kids to become strong, resilient, and productive members of society, but we don't give them the tools to get through challenging times.

Why is this so important? While everyone feels the effects of stress and anxiety during tumultuous times, adolescents are particularly vulnerable because of the developmental tornado happening inside them.

We expect teenagers to be mature enough to absorb and process emotionally turbulent news and events while also dealing with the day-to-day complexities of puberty. The reality is that they do not have the skills, perspective, or cognitive development to deal with it properly, causing many adolescents to retreat deeper within themselves. The result is a generation that is lonelier and more hopeless than previous ones.

For many of us, what we're feeling on the inside often comes out of us in a different way. For example, someone who feels stressed or out of control may turn it into rage against someone they love (I'm guilty). Someone who is embarrassed may end up in tears. Someone who feels rejected may end up belittling someone else. These responses often happen because we do not understand or cannot identify our emotional state.

It gets even more complicated when, even if your teen knows how they feel, they may be unable to articulate it. Communication skills are not always developed, or they may not feel they have a safe space to share.

While our kids face many traumatic events, such as violence in schools, bullying, or physical assaults, it's not just the big things we need to help our kids learn to manage. It's also the day-to-day stresses we experience in today's frenetic world.

We see it all the time. A student may be able to get an A in calculus, speak three languages, have the lead in the school musical, and gain entrance to a flagship college, but yet can't regulate their emotions, manage conflict, call to make an appointment, or approach an authority figure.

And as parents, we will spend hours shuttling our teens back and forth to activities, but we won't sit down with them and have tough conversations about managing and mitigating stress or protecting their mental health. There are countless stories of teens and young adults who break down and find themselves unable to get through and recover from a challenging situation because they have no gas left in their tank.

The problem lies with the fact that many teens don't understand that healthy coping mechanisms are available. Instead, they respond to internal negative feelings by wanting to avoid and numb any pain and discomfort they are experiencing. Many adolescents seek out and use quick fixes to quash their emotions, such as scrolling, cutting, shoplifting, vaping, bingeing, or seeking attention on social media. These types of activities may mask their feelings by numbing them, allowing them to postpone dealing with them, or providing a rush that temporarily replaces their discomfort. While this initially serves as a welcome distraction, these negative coping strategies often lead down a path to addictive behaviors, such as problems with alcohol, drugs, health disorders, or crime. (Reminder: unhealthy coping mechanisms can often turn into addictions, so you should seek professional help if you think your child needs better tools to cope.)

Coping mechanisms are an active way to process and deal with the emotions we experience about events that happen to us or around us. They are the things we can do to manage complex feelings, emotional distress, or even when we can't identify why we're upset. Without them, our stress and anxiety can turn into something more serious, such as rage, risk-taking behavior, isolation, or mental duress.

The thing about coping skills is we often only realize we need them once we're in the thick of a crisis. For example, you might handle the day-to-day stress of your life fine but find yourself ill-prepared to handle the emotions around a tragic event or a high-pressure situation. Or you may find that the daily annoyances of life, such as traffic, weather, or annoying Internet commenters, wear on you so heavily that you don't realize that when you blow up at the slow cashier, it's because you've been carrying stress for hours.

If our teens learn the importance of coping during these developmental years, they will always have these skills available to them for as long as they need them. They will be armed with the tools to manage whatever life throws at them, and more importantly, ensure they don't take their stress and emotions out on someone else. It is a gift that keeps on giving, and what can break the cycle of negative behavior in families.

HOW TO GET BUY-IN FROM YOUR TEENAGERS

Trust me, my teenagers have never once thanked me for trying to help them build healthy coping mechanisms, just like they have never said, "Gee, Mom, thanks for telling me to put down my phone. That curfew was awesome, too, and thanks for making me try Brussels sprouts."

I am not so naïve to think that you walk into your child's room one day and say, "Today's the day we're going to work on coping mechanisms!" I understand it doesn't work like that, and many tweens and teens will make you pay for merely suggesting they think about it.

But here's the thing: knowing how to deal with stress and manage your emotions through a difficult time can be the difference between surviving a tragedy and giving up. It can be the difference between getting through a breakup or having a breakdown. It can be the difference between thriving in a healthy relationship or thinking they deserve to be in an abusive one.

Adults who are volatile and explosive have trouble staying in school, maintaining relationships, keeping a job, or advancing their career. They are also more likely to engage in dangerous behaviors such as road rage or bullying.

It's that important. But how do you get your big kids to listen, and more importantly, implement?

Some adolescents may have mental health or medical conditions that require professional care or medication. If this is the situation for your child, there is no shame in it. You should treat it the same as addressing a genetic disease or other medical issue and it should be managed accordingly.

Other tweens and teens, however, just need guidance on managing this aspect of life—and you are not a failure if this is hard for you. If you've never seen emotional regulation or a healthy coping mechanism, you may have to work twice as hard to teach it to your kids. I know I did.

If you want your adolescents to address their stress levels and how they cope with it, you must have some tough conversations. Many tweens and teens find it incredibly challenging to talk about their feelings and will avoid it at all costs. They may lash out and tell you it's stupid. They may walk away or even slam a door.

Do not be deterred. This is life-changing stuff right here, and it may be hard on you both. What I have found is that many teens neither want nor possess the cognitive ability to understand their emotions. Many adolescents do not want to relive an experience that made them feel bad, so they either try to ignore it or numb their feelings in the hope they will dissipate. Many don't want to talk to their parents because they are convinced they don't understand, or they won't be appropriately acknowledged. And so the cycle continues.

For parents, there are ways we can help:

- **Model, model, and model again.** The most important thing we can do for our kids is show them firsthand how to cope with and handle challenging situations. That may mean stopping yourself before pouring a glass of wine after a hard day or grabbing your yoga mat instead of your phone when stressed. Remember, the goal isn't that they need to follow in your exact footsteps but to serve as a positive example that it is okay to make your emotional needs a priority.

- **Talk about the stress in your life.** Write down a list of the things you are currently managing and how you plan to cope. Share these with your family so you are all on the same page. Are you getting up earlier to exercise? Are you tracking your screen time? Did you start stashing peppermints in your purse so it would stop you from reacting negatively to your boss? Whatever you're doing, share that with your kids. You never know what may stick.

- **Make them the problem-solver.** While it would be great if you could just tell your big kid what to do and they would listen, I think we all know the likelihood of that happening. Instead, put the ball in their court. Ask them to share what they believe are some suitable coping mechanisms to help them manage their stress. When you circle back (which might take a few times until they actually do it), ask them about their plan to incorporate them into their daily or weekly routines. See if you can encourage them to practice a coping mechanism a few days a week.

- **Look at their schedule.** Overscheduling is a major problem for today's adolescents and college kids. Help your tweens and teens take a holistic look at their schedule and ensure there's some down-time on it. Sometimes we need to go as far as scheduling these self-care or coping activities for them.

- **Find appropriate peer role models.** I have a friend whose high-strung tween started meditating only after discovering that former University of Michigan quarterback J.J. McCarthy did it before games. Another teen I know started kickboxing after she heard British songstress Ellie Goulding did it to prevent panic attacks. Some teens may think coping strategies are just for middle-aged moms, until they find out their favorite athlete or celebrity uses them daily. On the flipside, after encouraging all three of my daughters to listen to podcasts or an audiobook to decompress, something I do regularly, each one shared that they struggled to listen and keep focus and preferred to listen to music instead. It's important they find what works for them.

- **Check in.** Sometimes, when our adolescents start retreating to their rooms, it's easy to assume that everything is fine, or they have nothing to discuss with you. It is essential to check in with your teen daily to assess their mental and physical status—yes, even if it annoys them. Make sure they are taking care of themselves and always know you are there for them if or when they want to talk. When one of my daughters went through a rough time, we had a number system. Each day when she returned from school, she would give me a number between one and five. Three or under meant she was managing well and taking care of herself. Four meant she was struggling and might need to talk. Five was red-alert and we booked time with her therapist or myself depending upon the problem. It helped me to take a step back from incessantly asking her how she was, and gave her an opportunity to assess her own well-being.

- **Post-game analysis.** If your tween or teen acts out, follow up with them later when they're calm. Ask them how they felt when upset and if they understand what caused their behavior. You can learn a lot if you take the time to do a self-analysis.

- **When necessary, insist.** My friend whose son is a competitive athlete found he struggled to control his anger at the end of a long day. His behavior put the entire house on edge. She finally had enough and insisted that whenever he started losing it on his younger siblings, he had to sit and count backward from 100. He did it begrudgingly at first, but now he implements it at home, school, and even on the field. Coping mechanisms are not a one-and-done exercise. Like building muscle or stamina, they need to be used regularly to get results.

PLAY THE LONG GAME

The most important thing to remember is that working on yourself is a process. Even those of us with the best of intentions can sometimes get off track.

The last few months before my twins graduated high school felt like drinking water from a firehose. Balancing my work schedule with the craziness of graduation season and raising another high schooler meant some things fell through the cracks, such as my daily morning walks to clear my head. It didn't take long for my stress to start bubbling into how I interacted with my family. At that moment, I recognized that the simple act of putting my feet to pavement outside transformed my entire attitude. The mere act of thinking about addressing my stress helped me cope more effectively.

It's also suitable for each family member to keep everyone accountable. When I notice one of my daughters spending a lot of time on her bed scrolling social media, I'll often ask her if she has any plans for a sewing project or baking something for me. I know if I comment about her screen time, she'll most likely get angry (triggered), but if I encourage her to do something creative, I'm supporting her coping mechanisms. For my husband, it's always leaving time for him to exercise, and you'll catch one of my twins always reading a book.

Whatever it takes.

MOVING FORWARD

I know this is a lot of information, and it may be tough to figure out where to start. I also appreciate that it can feel overwhelming, uncomfortable, and scary to start digging deep into your past (it's always easier to blame it on someone else). If you are wondering if you need to do a massive self-overhaul, there are some small things you and your family can do starting today to gain control of your emotions.

- **Write it down.** When you feel out of control, stop and write it down. Log what set you off or what you're feeling. It can be anything from dishes in the sink to a friend's snarky comment. You might want to identify when you burst into tears or lashed out at your dog. This activity allows you to start working backward and understand your triggers.

- **Focus on the why.** Ask yourself why certain behaviors might be bothering you, or why you may have reacted a certain way. Sometimes as parents we don't like to see a behavior in our kids that we have in ourselves. Adolescents may not want to address how hurtful it felt to be excluded or how embarrassed they were in gym class. Self-reflection is the gateway to controlling your emotions.

- **Determine what is typical adolescent behavior and what is behavior that you may need to correct.** We all know that sometimes teens do not keep their bedrooms neat. While teaching them how to clean and organize is good, we probably need to accept that some of it is typical developmental behavior for a kid their age. From an adult perspective, occasionally raising your voice or not responding in a certain way doesn't mean you must revamp your entire parenting style. Once you can discern between normal behavior and concerning behavior, you can learn how to control your reactions and emotions better. This doesn't mean you let your teen (or yourself) get away with bad behavior simply because it's age-appropriate, but it can help you react and respond to it more constructively.

- **Develop a plan.** You can't always avoid your triggers (especially when they live with you), but you can learn how to manage them. If you lose it every time your teen misses curfew, put a plan in writing that addresses it. Create specific rules and consequences on paper and make them sign it. Take the emotion out of it. If sibling fights put the entire family on edge, set some boundaries on how they can communicate with each other (no hitting, obscenities, cutting remarks, etc.) with consequences. The goal is to help everyone control their reactions.

- **Keep it kind and compassionate, always.** I had an open and honest discussion with my kids when I was going through a tough time. I told them that I wasn't acting like my best self, but I was working on it. Admitting that to them and seeing their positive response helped me become kinder and more compassionate, and I believe it brought us closer. Sometimes our big kids need to see our vulnerability and hear us admit our mistakes before they start understanding their own issues. Also, remember to be kind to yourself. We are all works in progress.

- **Find your calming techniques.** I used to think these were hokey, but now I'm like, don't knock it until you try it. When I know I'm on the edge, I walk. Even when it's a wet and cold Midwest afternoon, the simple act of being outside calms my head and heart. Find out what works and do it. It is time well spent.

CHAPTER TWELVE

THE HARDEST PART OF RAISING TEENS IS LETTING GO

Saying goodbye to your children and their childhood is much harder than all the pithy sayings make it seem. . . .It's not a death. And it's not a tragedy. But it's not nothing, either.
                    –Beverly Beckham, author and columnist

Sometime during your teen's senior year, things start getting very weird. It doesn't matter if your child is planning on going away to college, joining the military, attending a local vocational school, taking a gap year, getting a job, or has zero idea at all what they want to do next.

You are ending a chapter. And you may be devastated by the thought that your life is changing, excited about the future, or relieved that it will soon be over, but make no mistake, it is an ending—but it's not *the* end.

At some point, everything will be a countdown. Ten days before finals are done. Twenty-three days until graduation. Thirty-six days until family vacation. Seventy-four days until drop-off.

Those days will go by so fast and furious that they will take your breath away. They will be full of celebratory events, senior nights, and meetings to plan what's coming next. You'll be going through the motions to get through the frenzy of activity while pushing back the feeling that every day comes with a "last" attached to it.

The rush and range of emotions will be like nothing you've ever experienced. Pride, joy, fear, hope, worry, wonder, excitement, stress, and love.

You will try to stay present during this waning time when you still get a chance to see your child roll out of bed in the morning and catch a glance before they put their head down to sleep at night and whatever small moments you can grab during the in-between.

But it's not easy. Some kids "soil the nest" before they go, meaning they act so difficult that their parents want to push them out of their home. Sometimes we feel hurt and rejected because our kids only want to spend time with their friends or significant others. Sometimes we feel selfish or silly because we don't want our child to leave. And sometimes we feel guilty because we're relieved that this contentious and challenging time is ending.

I think I felt all those things and more during those last few months of senior year. Letting go is harder for some of us than it is for others.

THE DAY PARTY POTATOES BROKE ME

I thought I was handling my twins' senior year well. I didn't cry at an awards reception while my dear friend bawled like a baby. I didn't get teary like the parents I was sitting with at an admitted students' day at my daughter's future college. I even chuckled as I watched my husband choke up during senior night.

But then, one random Thursday, while preparing to host my daughter's last track team pasta dinner, I cried in my party potatoes.

Okay, maybe not *in* the party potatoes, but definitely while making them.

I've made party potatoes quite a bit the last few years. Some people know them as "funeral potatoes" or hashbrown casserole, but basically they're a staple for get-togethers in the Midwest and a must-have at team dinners for my daughter's track-and-field program. I could make them in my sleep.

But as I moved around my kitchen that afternoon, my mind filled with prom details for the weekend and getting to another daughter's soccer game and hoping my daughter's black shoes still fit for her orchestra concert and wondering how my child did on a big test and figuring out how to get the grandparents here for graduation in two weeks, and that simple dish started to feel heavy (and not just because of the block of cream cheese and tub of sour cream you use to make it). The weight of what was ending hit me like a ton of bricks as I placed the pan in the oven.

My life has been a whirlwind these last 18 years. They have been so full of baking and buying and attending and watching and rushing and playing and fixing and consoling and loving.

There have been scary moments spent in the emergency room or sleeping with my child because her mental health was suffering or feeling pieces of my heart breaking off because their hearts broke.

We've gone through grief because a fellow student died by suicide and fear because they were close to gun violence and worry as we watched them pull out of our driveway for the first time.

We've celebrated birthdays, achievements, and Sundays when we could all be together laughing until tears streamed down our faces. Those were the best.

During the craziness, you know that things are changing. Your kids outgrow your lap and suddenly ask to borrow your car. Your daughter starts stealing your clothes. Your baby now towers above you.

You long to reminisce about the first time your toddler saw the ocean or when she won 1,000 tickets at Chuck E. Cheese or when she beat all the boys at Field Day, but there isn't time because you're planning graduation parties and move dates and trying to remember if you ordered a boutonniere (you didn't).

It all went so fast, and suddenly I was standing in my kitchen making my last batch of party potatoes.

How did I get here? Did I miss it all in the doing? What happens now? As I wiped away the tears, I knew it went by in a blink. But I was there for it.

I remember my daughters' gapped smiles, the way they smelled at the end of a summer day, and the sound of their giggles when they were supposed to be asleep. I watched from the sidelines and cheered from the stands and clapped in the audience. We argued and made up a million times—and we loved so hard that our hearts grew bigger than we could have ever imagined.

And I made the party potatoes whenever I could.

I'm sad that this time in my life is over, but I'm also so glad I was part of it. It's grief and gratitude, joy and heartbreak, love and sorrow. I know I'm not any different. It's the life of every parent.

It's my party potatoes, and I'll cry if I want to.

It's okay if you cry, too.

THERE CAN ALWAYS BE SOMETHING TO LOOK FORWARD TO

My little neighborhood has an on-again, off-again book club that I love because it is full of women of all ages and perspectives.

One evening a few years back, my sweet neighbor asked how I was handling life with three kids in high school. As I rattled about the busyness, it dawned on me that I hadn't asked how she was doing.

"How are you handling the whole empty nest thing?" I asked.

And her eyes lit up. She shared that she was expecting her first grandchild later that year and could not wait.

She gushed about her daughter and the excitement of becoming grandparents. Her younger daughter had secured her first job and was recently engaged. My friend was helping her move to California. She joked that her son would never settle down, but it was okay because that meant he still came home for dinner. She volunteered on Wednesdays, helped with caring for a sick relative, and supported her husband's business. Her life was full even though the bedrooms in her house were now empty. In fact, she said, "I've never been so busy!"

I thought I would hear her say, "It all goes so fast," or "Enjoy it while you can." I thought she would lament about the past and missing what she had. But instead, she shared something so profound: "If you work at it, there's always something to look forward to when you have purpose, friends, and family."

Bam. Mic drop.

That's when I understood that an empty nest does not mean we stop loving and caring for the special people in our lives.

It's easy to get so caught up in the world of "lasts" that you miss where you are right now. And when you're in the thick of raising adolescents, hanging on by a thread, it's hard to imagine what life might look like down the road.

But that's precisely why we have to keep doing the work. Parenting is a long game. It's not 18 years, but as many moments as we are gifted, sometimes more and sometimes less. We are all on borrowed time.

I will not lie. It all goes fast and is not the same as when your kids are little. But honestly, in some ways, it is even better.

Sometimes, the space gained when your child is not living under your roof brings you closer. Sometimes, old wounds can heal with a bit of time.

Sometimes attitudes soften, habits change, young souls grow up, and old dogs can learn new tricks.

And sometimes they still need you in every way, and maybe even more. There is still a future to build, and we need to do the work today to ensure they know you want to be in their life tomorrow.

And that work means preparing ourselves for a life—a rich, beautiful, full life—that grows in lockstep with our children instead of centered around it.

We don't stop parenting simply because our kids no longer live in our homes.

There will be graduations and weddings and births. There will be vacations and celebrations and achievements. There will be times when they need me to hold them up and take them in, and there will be times when I need them to do the same.

My nest may soon be empty, but I choose to believe that my life will still be full because I will work on it.

HOW TO PREPARE FOR THE EMPTY NEST

Whether only one of your kids is leaving or the last one has just moved out, there are some things you can do to make the transition a little easier.

- **Make plans before your kids leave.** Although most of us want to spend all our time with our kids before they move out, it's good to see what your life could look like when they are no longer living with you. Whether going back to work, taking a class, joining a club, or volunteering, filling some time gaps can help ease the transition. One idea that another parent who is a decade ahead of me shared is that you don't have to stop contributing to the activities that you shared with your kids, which is why she still volunteers at the football concessions stand each season. I've heard some parents still coach Little League, attend school concerts and plays, or start substitute teaching. Fill the cracks in your heart in whatever way you can.

- **Set expectations.** Sometimes, the transition can be more challenging because parents and their big kids do not share the same expectations on communication. Some teens will call home daily, while others may only check in after several requests for proof of life. Some may not consider coming home for Thanksgiving and Christmas to be reasonable. Some don't like to talk on the phone. Have a frank conversation with your child *before* they leave home about the expectations, so you don't make the communication you do have filled with arguments.

- **Map out your first visit before they leave.** If possible and not a strain on your budget, plan your first visit and put it on the calendar. Whether it's a scheduled family weekend at college, a break from basic training, or a trip home for Thanksgiving, mark it down. Seeing it on paper will ease the pain of not having a return trip or visit on the books.

- **Empty nest syndrome is a real thing.** You are not alone if you struggle with controlling your emotions regarding your children moving out of your home. Some parents find the new family dynamic difficult and debilitating. Don't listen to people who mock and minimize your feelings. Engaging a mental health therapist or support group can help get you through this time. One mom shared that she cried for a month after dropping her only child off at college. It took a few months of therapy to work through some abandonment issues she had been dealing with her entire life. Another mom told me that her entire family struggled when the eldest left for the military, but especially her other two children. Managing their strong reactions and her own grief taxed her emotionally and physically. Have a plan and coping mechanisms to help get you through it.

- **Talk to other parents who get it.** Everyone deals with things in different ways. My closest friends all have younger kids who were still keeping them busy, so while we talked, I felt like our heartache was on different levels. One day, while grocery shopping, I ran into another mom I had barely seen since our kids were in elementary school. Her son was in my twins' graduating class, but they didn't run in the same crowd. We spoke for 25 minutes about how we both were struggling and fighting some anxiety as graduation loomed before us. Despite not having much in common, we were both fighting the same emotional battle. I like to think we helped each other that day in the condiment aisle. Keep your heart open and eyes up because you never know who can help you through a tough time.

- **Share your feelings with your kids.** One night, I drove my daughter home from a school event. She was sharing some "tea" regarding some drama she had heard about, and we laughed at how ridiculous it sounded. She told me that she was glad not to have to deal with some of the issues that impacted her during high school anymore. That's when I decided to tell her, "I'm so glad you get a fresh start, but I'm just sad because I'm going to miss you so much too. I've really enjoyed the last few months."

  Everyone has a different philosophy on what to share with their kids. Some people believe you don't say anything so that they don't feel bad about leaving, and some share so much that teens are wracked with guilt. I believe it's okay to be honest and vulnerable with your big kids because you never know what you'll get in return. When my daughter responded, "Same, Mom. Same," well, it made my night.

- **Take care of yourself.** When we don't have others to care for, we may stop taking care of ourselves. Maintaining self-care and using healthy coping mechanisms can be so important. Make sure you're eating healthy, exercising, and getting enough sleep. I also recommend journaling during this time so you can address your feelings.

I've found that each season of parenting comes with new surprises. I still miss my kids, but even though they aren't under my roof, I'm thankful we have many ways to stay connected. I send funny dog reels through Instagram and utilize our family group text and Facetime whenever I can. My husband and daughter play in a fantasy football league, and we've been able to visit more than I thought.

It's not the way it was, but it's not the end either. And sometimes it's even better.

CHAPTER THIRTEEN

HOW TO LOVE
A TEENAGER

You either married your greatest test in life or you gave birth to it or you may find your biggest test when you look into the mirror.

—Dr. John Lewis Lund ("The Communications Doctor"), relationship counselor and author of *How to Hug a Porcupine*

think it's essential that I take a moment to let you know that I think all three of my teenagers are awesome. Despite all my missteps, emotional baggage, and internal issues, my kids turned into some fantastic humans I admire greatly. I believe they will change the world.

No, really. I know I'm writing an entire book about how challenging these teenage years are, and I'm sharing with you all the problems I've had while raising them, but man, my kids are incredible. It is my honor to be a part of their lives. In fact, when I was struggling to come up with the right title for this chapter, my youngest suggested "Everything I Learned from My Awesome Daughter," which was catchy, but we decided to go in another direction.

But in all seriousness, as much as I care for and admire my teens, raising them also felt like living with three intelligent, adorable, lovable porcupines who reside in the middle of a dangerous forest full of things ready to take you down at any moment. It reminds me of the movie *Jumanji*.

No big deal.

Porcupines are solitary, slow-moving mammals that keep to themselves. Their quills lie flat against their body unless they feel threatened, which they then will erect to scare predators. If they need to defend themselves, they swing their spiny tails until they feel safe or they insert sharp quills into their opponent. They are nocturnal, can sleep anywhere, and need personal space.

Does any of this sound familiar?

WHAT TO DO WHEN YOU DON'T KNOW WHAT TO DO NEXT

If you've made it this far, you may feel overwhelmed with information. I lived through most of the teen years already, and spent a good chunk of time working on myself. If you are at the cusp of this journey or are mentally and physically exhausted from feeling like a failure, you may not know where to start.

Let's break it down.

We need to talk more about how tricky it is to navigate these relationships with almost-adults who are desperate for independence. Even when you have a solid relationship, these porcupines will show their quills when they feel their back is up against the wall.

Like how do you handle it when your teen stays out past curfew and never checks in? In a few short months, they might be living on their own, enlisting in the military, or paying their own way, yet you want to ground them.

How do you talk to a young person who seems to cry at the drop of a hat, slams their bedroom door, or refuses to come out of their room? How do you make your son feel better when he gets bullied incessantly and won't talk about it? What do you say to the teen who seems to keep lying for no good reason except they can?

What do you do when things spiral out of control and you have a teen engaging in risky behavior, such as vaping, drugs, or alcohol?

Or what do you do when your teen comes to you and says, "I'm scared I might hurt myself."

Even if you know your kids are doing well, and you know your kids have great hearts, it's still tricky and complicated and exhausting—and you never know if you're getting it right at the time. But here are a few things we must remember. Teens are:

- Navigating a complex world. Many do not yet have the communication or emotional skills to process what is happening around them.
- Dealing with a changing body, hormones, and brain development.
- Challenging boundaries so they can figure out where the lines and limits are.
- Learning to manage stressful situations like academics, peer pressure, romantic relationships, work-life balance, and plans for what they will do next.
- Figuring out their wants and how to care for themselves. They often do not get enough sleep, don't know how to protect their mental health, and may not understand the world around them.
- Trying to determine their identity and gain control over their life.
- Developing perspective on issues.
- Building resilience through mistakes and failures.
- Finding their place in a world without their parents as the center of it.

It is tricky but mission-critical stuff. And this means they will make bad choices, react poorly, and maybe even say awful things to those they love the most.

And if you find your porcupine shows you their quills more than you'd like or maybe even swings its tail at you to release a few barbs, it doesn't mean you're failing. It means you're doing your best with the kid before you, and you might have to try something new tomorrow.

YOU CAN START FRESH EVERY DAY

When writing about the struggle of raising adolescents, I often have people point out what we "should have" focused on when the child was younger.

I always want to respond, "Thanks, Captain Obvious, but here we are today. My crystal ball must not have worked in those early years." I mean, what a hopeless message we're giving to parents of tweens and teens.

But what I want you to remember, what I hope gets you through these long days and these even longer nights, is the fact that as long as you both have breath in your body and love in your heart, you can work on the relationship with your child.

If you dig deep into yourself. If you work on your responses. If you understand your triggers. If you remain flexible and open-minded. If you hold onto the belief in your child's unconditional goodness. If you love your kid hard and love yourself harder.

You can move forward, and that's not just something. It's everything.

THERE IS STILL TIME

It is never too late to set boundaries. It's never too late to change your house rules. It's never too late to have another conversation. It's never too late to love them through the hard parts. It's never too late to address your past issues or work on healing your past trauma. It's never too late to find gratitude. It's never too late to try a different approach.

It is not easy to love a porcupine. It's dangerous, and these animals will make it extremely challenging for you to do so. They are designed that way to protect themselves. They will use every tool at their disposal to avoid what they believe is harmful contact, including slinging their tail to stick their opponent with sharp quills, biting, releasing unpleasant smells from their glands, or running away. They will act like they want nothing to do with anyone else, but that's not necessarily the case.

There is a well-kept secret that the underside of a porcupine has no quills. If you can approach one just right, you can scoop it up. You just need to know a few secrets.

While this season of parenting can be challenging and lonely, know you are not alone. So many of us are feeling it—and we don't see you failing; we see you trying. And that is something.

If you're at the end of the rope with your porcupine and tired of getting hurt, your gut may tell you to stay away. Let your tween or teen huddle in their room so you can avoid their hurtful barbs and keep away from their dangerous tails.

And I get that. Sometimes we're exhausted from this world, and taking on someone who is lashing out or makes it difficult to be around feels like it may break us.

But one thing I've learned from speaking to parents on the other side of the teenage years, one thing I've learned from my journey, is we always have a little more love to give. It doesn't mean we should be a human punching bag, but we can't give up on our kids. We can learn how to pick them up and hold them close.

Your relationship may not look how you want it to right now, but by leaning into it today, it may change tomorrow, next month, or five years from now. It is an investment that can pay off with the most beautiful returns.

When you feel like a failure and don't know what else to try, the following pages give a few last bits of advice I've received over the years. These won't solve all your problems, but when you feel like nothing is working, these ideas may help you to stay in the game.

STAY IN THE OPEN

I hate the sound of the click of my teen's bedroom door. It reminds me of the impenetrable closing of a bank vault where everything I want lies behind it, unavailable to me—and it's a constant reminder that my kids often would rather be where I am not.

When this first started happening, when my kids would come home late in the evening after being at a practice or study session or out with friends, I simply retreated to my room earlier and earlier. I would watch a show upstairs in my pajamas or work on a project. I figured if my kids wanted something, they would find me down the hall.

But they never sought me out. They never came in to chat or to tell me about their day. They would grab a snack and shout a hello as they walked past my room toward their own. I wouldn't say I liked the silence, but I also tried to respect their privacy.

One evening, I was in the kitchen making some chicken noodle soup for a friend who had recently had surgery. I decided to pop in a batch of cookies we had in the freezer from a fundraiser as well. One of my daughters walked in after a long cross-country practice and plopped herself down at the kitchen counter. We started chatting, and I was shocked when she took out her laptop to finish her math assignment instead of heading to her room.

A few moments later, one of my other kids clomped down the stairs to fill her water bottle. The next thing I knew, she was waiting to grab a cookie from the oven. Then, miracle of miracles, my third child walked in from a friend's house, and she sat down at my counter, too. I made another batch of cookies, and we hung out for 55 glorious minutes, laughing and catching up on our day.

Then they unceremoniously went to their respective rooms and shut their doors. But I felt connected, and our hearts and bellies were full.

After that, I stopped retreating to my room early. I sat right on the couch, so my three teens had to walk past me whenever they went to the kitchen, up to their rooms, or to grab something off the printer. Sometimes they walked by looking stressed or annoyed, and I gave them a smile. Sometimes they would plop on the couch for a quick opportunity to complain about a teacher or an assignment. Sometimes, if I were very lucky, they'd ask me to put on a show we'd watch together.

I kept at it. Even after all three had their licenses, I always offered to drive. I gave them permission to have their friends over whenever they wanted. I stayed in the kitchen or the living room whenever possible. It was a lot of waiting around, just in case, but it was so worth it.

As my friend and fellow writer Kerry Foreman says, raising teens is full-time availability for a part-time job.

It was worth it because they knew I was ready if they wanted to talk. They knew I was watching and witnessing their comings and goings and everything in between. They knew by sitting on the couch, in my car, or at the kitchen counter, I cared. They knew that no matter what was going on behind that bedroom door, I was available on the other side of it, whether they needed me or not.

They don't make it easy. There will be times when your very existence annoys them. They might vape in their room or want privacy with their significant other. They might not have the emotional energy to spend on you. They may even think they hate you.

But no matter what is going on with them, you can always be there for them, and that is something positive in their lives.

DATE YOUR BIG KIDS

Here is a fact that I didn't realize about teenagers. You can put down a child one night, and without warning, a different person can wake up in your home the following day.

That person may have different interests, opinions, and tastes about every single thing. They might suddenly tower over you and appear unrecognizable. They might start calling you by your first name. They might have a romantic interest or start discussing why they can't wait to move out and live independently.

And it can be a shock.

You might serve them their absolute favorite spaghetti-and-meatballs dinner, and they casually say, "Oh, I'd rather have Gigi Hadid's Spicy Vodka Pasta." (True story.)

Or they may suddenly drink a caramel oat milk iced espresso instead of chocolate milk on Saturday mornings. (Also a true story.)

Or they may be working on a new song on their guitar to jam out with friends instead of wanting to play the clarinet in the band.

Or they may suddenly douse themself in some drugstore cologne.

Or they may no longer want you to hug and kiss them goodnight, which shatters your heart into a million pieces.

The essence of those kids will still be there. You will hear it in a giggle when someone says "poop," or you may see it in their round faces when they fall asleep on the couch, but mostly the change happens when you blink.

So you have to get to know this new version of your kids, and the best way to do that is to date them.

In the book *Outliers,* a fantastic read by Malcolm Gladwell about the opportunities kids have to succeed, the premise is that great achievers weren't born that way. Instead, they put in the most hours. Gladwell suggests that the key to success in any field is to practice the task for at least 10,000 hours.

Does that mean I suggest you spend 10,000 hours getting to know your newly minted adolescent? Well, not exactly. But spending quality time getting to know them can positively impact your relationship.

I say "date" because there is something purposeful about it. Sometimes, because we spend time driving our kids back and forth from activities or we sit in the same room, we think that is enough. But a date is intentional. It's a special event that allows us to learn about the other person, ask about their likes and dislikes, or do something fun together. With your tween or teen, it is the perfect opportunity to learn their new interests.

Most importantly? It builds connection and trust. The goal is to show your big kid that you are open to this next version of themselves and accept them. It could be as short as a coffee date or a weekend trip, but it will be time worth spending.

DO THE UNEXPECTED

One of the greatest gifts we can give our teenagers is the ability to care for themselves. It builds their confidence in an unsettled world.

But I also believe that when your teen is prickly, when you don't know what's going on in that head of theirs, when they are at their most moody and sullen, you have an opportunity to show them you can always be kind and loving—no matter what.

One time, my daughter was struggling with a personal problem where I knew just a few details. She was lashing out at the entire family, and even our dog was avoiding her. We had about enough of her attitude, and for three days, she isolated herself in her room whenever she was at home.

Each day, while she was at school, I tried to do something kind for her. I folded her laundry and put it away. Another day, I made her favorite meal and put some aside for her lunch. Another time I changed her sheets and made her bed.

It wasn't a reward for her bad behavior. She didn't even thank me for doing those acts until a few days later. Still, I wanted her to know that even when things aren't right between us, or when she feels like the world is out to get her, I'll be there for her, no matter what.

My hope in extending kindness in response to her unsavory behavior is to remind her that I love her at her best and also when she's hard to love. She can always count on me—even when she's going through a tough time.

Acts of kindness during challenging times are as much for me as for my kids. It can take my mind off the problem or feeling I'm experiencing and give me some control in a challenging situation. And it makes me feel good, improving my mindset and responses.

There is a difference between swooping in and saving our kids and being kind. There are moments when we need them to experience natural consequences and times when they need kindness and compassion. The goal is always to help them grow through whatever they are going through.

PERSPECTIVE IS EVERYTHING

Even the most level-headed teenager can lose their mind sometimes over something that we, as parents, know is not a big deal. And the worst thing we can do is tell them that it is not a big deal.

Live by this motto: *Their perspective is small, but their feelings are big.*

Whatever it is, it is a big deal to them because they have zero life experience at this point in the game.

Whether it's a crush who hasn't texted them back, a bad grade on a test, losing a big game, or not having the right shoes, it doesn't matter. In their heads at that moment, without any perspective, it is a gigantic deal.

We might know that their crush is a butt head and that the grade won't change their life course and there will be another chance to go to the playoffs and there are a million other pairs of shoes that will go with their dress, but they don't know that *yet*.

We may think we're helping by offering perspective, but what your teen hears is, "You don't get me. You don't understand. You don't care."

Dismissing or diminishing their problems can create a rift between you and your child that may be hard to repair.

The adolescent years come with a lot of drama, but our kids need to learn what their role in it is. It comes from experiencing it. We've already gone to our show and know how it turns out. It is their turn.

Our job is to listen, affirm, and guide when asked. It can make you want to pull your hair out, and you will bite your tongue off to keep from saying anything, especially when you know what they're talking about is silly, dangerous, or annoying. But the end goal is to keep the lines of communication open.

Sometimes what seems like complaining about something ridiculous may be processing something they don't quite understand yet. Or they might only be sharing the tip of the iceberg of a bigger problem, and how you react could determine if you get the whole story.

I have a friend who has raised four great kids. She told me that the most critical job of a parent of teens is to bear witness to their problems, no matter how ridiculous they may seem, and believe in their importance. Sometimes the best words you can utter are "I'm sorry that happened. That sucks."

My friend and motherhood mentor Shelby Spear says the goal is always to help our kids move through their problems, not surrender to them.

We do that by acknowledging them, no matter what.

THEY HAVE TO MESS UP TO GROW UP

Parenting coach Amiee Carlton (@amieecarlton_coaching on Instagram) uses a phrase that I love: "Teens have to mess up to grow up." That is such a mic-drop statement.

Our instinct is always to protect our kids, and as they enter their tween and teen years, we do this even more because we feel like the stakes are high. We feel that to be "good" parents, our kids must never make a mistake. We confuse bad choices with bad kids.

We may not want them to repeat the missteps of our youth, or we may not want them to miss out on an opportunity. We may feel guilty for things we have done (or haven't done) or want them to keep up with others.

But in doing so, we rob our big kids of the ability to learn from their mistakes, build resilience, become good decision-makers, resolve conflicts, and grow as people.

Trust me, I'm not so good at this part, the letting go and letting them fail.

I hear all the advice intellectually, but my heart wants me to go in a different direction, bring them back close to me, and hold on tighter. I fight my own anxiety by controlling what I can, by taking action, and by doing. I want them to have all the things and experiences that I missed out on.

But at what cost for my children and their futures? So we must walk behind them.

Amiee also has said this: "We are saving our teens from their mistakes repeatedly in the hope that we can love them into taking some responsibility for their lives." But life doesn't work like that.

The problem is that our kids can only master something if they experience it, and this means they need to deal with the challenges and hardships of life on their own, with us staying available to guide and help as needed.

Sometimes, as parents today, we feel it has to be all one way or another, but there is a happy medium. Giving our tweens and teens some control over their decisions, trusting that they may know what is best for them, and allowing them to solve a problem before stepping in is basically like a self-confidence booster shot.

While there are times when I want to tell one of my three children, "I told you so," or "You should have listened to me the first 50 times," I've found that we both feel better and grow closer when I can say, "I knew you would figure it out. Way to go!"

STAY IN THE VILLAGE

One of my first viral posts on social media occurred about seven years ago. Entitled "No One Told Me How Lonely It Was to Raise Teenagers," it was shared hundreds of thousands of times on Facebook. I still receive messages about it. It was the moment that I realized that so many of us were feeling the exact same way. It's why I wrote this book.

There are many reasons to close off our circles during these turbulent times of raising tweens and teens. We need to protect their privacy. We don't want judgment or snide comments. We are embarrassed or ashamed. We are unsure of whom to trust. We are swamped trying to manage our full lives. We are exhausted from the mental and physical load that modern parenting requires.

But the truth is, we need each other.

We need to be more open to discussing big issues without sharing every small detail. We need to give each other permission to say, "This is hard, and I always feel like I'm doing it wrong." We need to remember that we never know what someone else is going through behind closed doors.

We need to stay in the village, maybe not in the same way when we sat together at holiday concerts and pickup lines, but in acknowledging the struggles, offering private messages of support, and stopping gossip in its tracks.

That also means, whenever possible, believing the best of other parents.

If someone comes to you with information about your child, thank them. It does not mean it's true, and it does not mean you need to act on it, but we shouldn't be defensive. We have created a culture of noninterference when it comes to raising our tweens and teens when instead we need healthy boundaries and open communication.

And when you see a teenager doing something great, tell them and maybe shoot an email to the parents, too. It may be the only kind word either of them receive that day.

BE VULNERABLE

Vulnerability is my superpower. I thrive on connection, and sharing stories is my favorite thing in the world. It doesn't mean I believe everyone should blast their private information all over the Internet, but it does mean stretching yourself to acknowledge and share what you're going through with someone else in your life.

The two messages I receive the most from parents are "Thank you for sharing so I feel less alone" and "I thought I was the only one." I don't write for accolades or attention. I do it because I know what it feels like to go through tough times and have someone extend a hand to me in support. I hope you seize the opportunity if you can do that for someone else in whatever way possible.

The relationships with my three daughters are not perfect. I've struggled in my marriage. I've had friendships end and people who have chosen not to prioritize me in their lives. I've made a million mistakes. I worry a lot and second-guess all the time. I never know what I'm doing.

But I also see progress. I received a phone call from my daughter at college asking for my opinion (*gasp!*). I had a tough conversation with another child about a misunderstanding. My youngest always asks me to go for coffee. Sure, it might be because I pay, but I think she likes the conversation too.

I feel more comfortable in my skin and more focused in my day. I find peace—not all the time, but enough to know I've grown up just as much as my three girls over the last decade.

I see my daughters for everything they are—the good, the bad, and the ugly—and I love them deeply. I hope I'm raising them to love others in the same way. I know I'm thankful for the love and encouragement they give their father and me in everything we pursue.

Dr. Brené Brown says this about vulnerability: "In our culture, we associate vulnerability with emotions we want to avoid, such as fear, shame, and uncertainty. Yet we too often lose sight of the fact that vulnerability is also the birthplace of joy, belonging, creativity, authenticity, and love."

You don't need to post your stories on social media like I do or write a book about all the ways you messed up.

But I hope we keep being honest about how hard it is to raise teenagers in today's world. I hope we keep sharing our stories with friends, neighbors, and other parents we meet so they feel less alone. I hope we try to connect when we know someone has hit a rough patch, and we bravely and compassionately reach out when we know someone's child is struggling. I hope we offer unlimited grace to other parents, teens, and ourselves.

We should keep showing our kids that vulnerability isn't a sign of weakness but a show of strength, self-actualization, and an opportunity for personal growth.

My emotions may be on my sleeve, but my head is clear, and my heart is open.

And that's the kind of mom I want to give my kids.

ONE FINAL NOTE

It's hard to have an unconditional belief in your teenager that they will rise to the occasion, especially when you're going through a challenging time with them.

But letting them try, knowing you believe they can do it? That's when the magic happens, and the endless tug-of-war relaxes.

Our job is to help them be the best version of themselves, but the path they take to get there must be their own. Help them by trying to become the best version of yourself, because it's never too late to try.

And if we get out of their way and let them become the person they were meant to be, the hope is we'll keep a relationship that lasts far longer than this short, challenging season.

All we can do is love the kid in front of us while letting them go at the same time.

And feeling it all.

Love hard.

ACKNOWLEDGMENTS

To the team at The Bindery literary agency, and specifically Alex Field, thank you for finding me on social media and believing that I could write a book.

To the team at Jossey-Bass, thank you so much for your patience, thoughtfulness, and belief in my words. You are consummate professionals and made the process easy and enjoyable. Sophie, thank you for keeping me on track, and Tom, thank you for the encouraging way you guided my manuscript. And to Amy Fandrei, thank you for holding my hand through this entire process and getting who I am. I look forward to continuing to support each other throughout our careers, but I also am grateful for your friendship.

One of the hardest parts of writing this book was also maintaining the integrity of the blog over at *Parenting Teens & Tweens*. I am enormously grateful to our amazing little business-team-that-could, including Christine, Karen, Kristen, Kimberly, my dear friend Michelle who was my sounding board for this book in the beginning, and of course, my business partner and sister from another mister, Kira Lewis. I love what we are building, and I love doing it with all of you.

To the women in my life who constantly build me up, including my Gator girls, the Queenagers, my Landon neighbors, Jill and Denise back in the Burgh, my colleagues in the online publishing and social media world (special shout-out to Amy Betters-Midtvedt and Mikala Albertson for helping me as early readers while writing their own books), and everyone who takes the time to shoot me a message, stop me at a soccer game, or send a note sharing that they loved something I wrote, there are no words to express my love and appreciation. Thank you.

To my *Whitney Fleming Writes* social media community, I am so proud of what we built together. I know that this book deal is largely because of your support, and I never take that for granted. I also need to send a shout-out to my personal friends on Facebook who encouraged me to start a blog nearly a decade ago, and to the friends of my kids who like my memes on Insta. It makes me smile every time I see a heart from you.

To my extended family, and particularly my in-laws Linda and Rich, thank you for all your support. I know it's been tough to understand what I do sometimes, but you've always encouraged me to go after my dreams.

To my mom, Sally, I will never be able to find the words to let you know how much love and respect I have for you. I'm lucky to have you as a parent but even more as a friend.

To my dad, Jim. You've been gone for two decades now, and yet your voice is always in my ear. I hope I've made you proud.

There would be no book on my experiences raising teenagers if it weren't for the three beautiful turkeys who call me "Mom." To Payton, thank you for inspiring me with the dedication and passion you put into chasing your dreams. Your excitement for this book helped push me to the finish line. To Olivia, thank you for always reminding me that empathy and kindness are superpowers. I know that one day I will be reading *your* book. And to Cam, I'm so appreciative of your support and listening to me complain about how hard it is to write a book day in and day out. I will miss our coffee runs.

Finally, thank you to my husband, Mark, for loving me so much that you are willing to put up with our unruly and disobedient dog, Jax. And also for supporting me in every crazy thing I do. I'm looking forward to writing our next chapter.

ABOUT
THE AUTHOR

Whitney Fleming is passionate about telling stories that help others feel less alone. As a writer, social media consultant, mother, and advocate, she puts an authentic and empathetic voice to issues such as parenting, mental health, grief, marriage, and midlife. With a combined one million-plus followers, she co-owns and manages the successful blog *Parenting Teens & Tweens* (www.parentingteensandtweens.com) and is the voice behind the popular social media accounts @WhitneyFlemingWrites. She is the author of the Amazon best-selling book *Loving Hard When They're Hard to Love* and has been published in six anthologies. Whitney lives in the Chicago suburbs with her husband, three teenage daughters, and her unruly dog, Jax.